Creating
Safe
Schools

Series Editors:
John T. Greer
Donn W. Gresso

Principals Taking
ACTION
Series

Joint publications of
THE NATIONAL ASSOCIATION OF SECONDARY SCHOOL PRINCIPALS
and
CORWIN PRESS, INC.

Rethinking Student Discipline
Alternatives That Work
    Paula M. Short, Rick Jay Short and Charlie Blanton

Thriving on Stress for Success
    Walter H. Gmelch and Wilbert Chan

Creating Safe Schools
What Principals Can Do
    Marie Somers Hill and Frank W. Hill

Marie Somers Hill
Frank W. Hill

Creating
Safe
Schools

What Principals Can Do

CORWIN PRESS, INC.
A Sage Publications Company
Thousand Oaks, California

We dedicate this book to our parents:
Gene, Alice, Sam, and Betty

For information address:

Corwin Press, Inc.
A Sage Publications Company
2455 Teller Road
Thousand Oaks, California 91320

SAGE Publications Ltd.
6 Bonhill Street
London EC2A 4PU
United Kingdom

SAGE Publications India Pvt. Ltd.
M-32 Market
Greater Kailash I
New Delhi 110 048 India

Printed in the United States of America

Library of Congress Cataloging-in-Publication Data

Hill, Marie Somers.
    Creating safe schools : what principals can do / Marie Somers Hill,
Frank W. Hill.
        p.   cm. — (Principals taking action)
    Includes bibliographical references and index.
    ISBN 0-8039-6147-2 (alk. paper). — ISBN 0-8039-6148-0 (pbk: alk. paper)
    1. School violence—United States—Prevention. 2. Schools—United
States—Safety measures. 3. School principals—United States.   I. Hill, Frank
W. (Frank William) II. Title. III. Series: Principals taking action series.
LB3013.3.H56 1994
371.7'82—dc20   94-21621
                                                                          CIP

94 95 96 97 98   10 9 8 7 6 5 4 3 2 1

Corwin Press Production Editor: Yvonne Könneker

Contents

List of Boxes

Preface

While giving us great satisfaction, the settings in which the two of us have been principals have nevertheless also generated stressful dreams, often pulling us from sleep in the middle of the night. Here and there our struggles to find answers to dilemmas at school wake us at 3:00 a.m., and we find ourselves in a cold sweat trying to clear our heads. At the same time, we try not to lose the strands of a solution we were attempting to construct. Undercurrents of potential violence are a too prevalent theme of these nightmares for principals.

Other realities hit us at midday: Upon request, a student relinquishes a weapon, and with a moment to reflect on the event, we wonder, "What if he hadn't? . . . What if shots had sprayed across campus? . . . What if . . . ?"

Daily news accounts and statistics from national studies bombard us with shocking portrayals of violence within schools. Steadily increasing probabilities that violence can occur within and around any school are propelling all of us to examine our own settings.

What can be done to prevent violence from invading our schools? We need to take some comfort in being several steps closer to a solution by just asking the question. Your willingness to read this book also makes you a principal with the foresight and dedication to create a safer school.

The pages ahead offer a variety of approaches to consider. Some strategies are taken from research, demographics, and various writings, but most are from our own experiences as principals. We have been principals in 13 different schools, ranging from 130 students in an alternative setting to 700 suburban elementary school students in the northeast to an inner-city urban high school with 3,000 students in the southeast. Our range of experiences, as well as our efforts and the wisdom of others to seek solutions, are summarized in the chapters ahead.

Chapter 1 reviews primary sources of violence that increasingly challenge our culture. The mission of schools is challenged by children from dysfunctional families unable to provide for them. Woven into the cause and effect of dysfunctional families is the problem of drugs and chemical dependency. Accessibility of weapons, replacement of traditional families by organized gangs, clashes of difference among our economic strata, and acceptance of violence by the media mesh to form a complex issue.

Chapter 2 explores the reality that violence is not just an urban issue in poor neighborhoods. Three examples of different schools at pivotal points offer you the opportunity to stop time and anticipate the best possible solutions. You also have the luxury of hindsight to back up and put strategies into place that give the principals dealing with precarious situations needed advantages.

Suggestions in Chapter 3 address nine approaches to creating a safer school setting for the school leader to consider. Leadership expectations and behaviors are powerful factors in creating a climate that rejects violence.

Students are often overlooked as essential components in combating violence in schools. Chapter 4 explores eight alternatives that can be implemented to involve students in creating safer schools. The entire learning environment is strengthened when students are involved in the workings and governance of the school and classroom.

Chapter 5 addresses coalitions within the community. Involving the community, and most specifically parents, in school activities also sets a tone prohibiting aggressiveness. When the principal finds ways to facilitate the integration of community services, concomitant benefits are generated for students, families, and the school. Suggestions for and examples of successful parent involvement programs are also found in Chapter 3.

Responsibility for creating safer schools does not rest solely with the principal. Chapter 6 explores the assistance that should be expected from the central office. Policy implementation, collaborative planning, and proactive approaches must be initiated by the central office to support administrative efforts at each school.

The school facility contributes to escalating or de-escalating a violent environment. Chapter 7 outlines a building and campus approach to stemming crime. Subtle to very overt approaches are outlined for you to custom select the combination that best fits your needs.

Chapter 8 presents ideas for use in proactively planning reactions to disastrous situations. A selection of this last chapter is also devoted to techniques to use if a tragic situation does occur in your school.

The volatile, destructive combination of students and weapons has moved nearly every national educational organization to action. They are offering their united efforts to schools to counter violence in a variety of ways. The National Association of Secondary School Principals (NASSP), for example, issued a contract to stop violence to each of its 40,000 members. The contract as well as a press release and proclamations by NASSP are included for your use as resources at the end of this book.

Schools have long been regarded as safe havens, even in the toughest settings. Achieving effective communities of learners as safe havens is the challenge faced by all principals. We hope that ideas offered in the following pages provide alternatives to the challenges confronting every principal. "Sweet dreams."

About the Authors

Marie Somers Hill is Associate Professor in the Department of Educational Leadership and Policy Analysis at East Tennessee State University. She has served as a faculty member at the University of Central Florida and Wesleyan College and was a principal and teacher for 16 years. Her articles have been published in many professional journals, including *NASSP Bulletin, Principal, The Journal of School Leadership,* and *Psychology Today.* She serves as correspondent for *DESIGN for Leadership* and is on the editorial board of *Research in the Schools.*

She has conducted professional development workshops throughout the country for Phi Delta Kappa and various school districts. She has been a guest lecturer at the University of the Yucatan. Her academic interests include the principalship, leadership preparation programs, and teacher leadership. She received her undergraduate degree from Glenville State College and her graduate degrees from Rollins College and Mississippi State University. She has completed postdoctoral studies at Vanderbilt University and the University of Alaska.

Frank W. Hill is the Director of Johnson Academy, which serves special needs students from developmentally delayed preschoolers through young adults pursuing a high school diploma. For more than two decades, he has been a principal in Tennessee, Pennsylvania, Florida, and Delaware. He has served as an adjunct faculty member at East Tennessee State University.

At a variety of conferences, he has presented programs on approaches to supporting at-risk students. He has also developed alternative funding through foundation grants. His undergraduate degree from Kutztown University was followed with a master's degree from Salisbury State College and other graduate work from Vanderbilt University, University of Delaware, Temple University, and Rowan College.

Building Principals' Awareness

Sources of Violence in Schools

T he North American culture is increasingly becoming a violent
culture. A review of each evening's lead news contains a sad
retrospection of a day filled with the violent, harmful behavior of one
person or group against another. Yellow crime scene tape creates
abstracts on concrete of former living beings.

Even the sports news recounts poor judgment and unethical esca-
pades. Often the longest sports segments highlight blow-by-blow
accounts of our national sports heroes settling disagreements on the
court or field. Violence is commonly accepted not only as a way to
solve conflict but even as a way to celebrate. What would a national
championship be without a post-win riot? Two people were murdered
and 682 arrested following the 1993 Chicago Bulls' National Basket-
ball Association victory. *Sports Illustrated* lamented that the total dam-
ages in Montreal reached $10 million following a hockey championship.

These incidents are all evidence of a grim ritual in which we
celebrate major sports triumphs by turning our cities' meanest

streets even meaner, filling them with feral packs of kids and criminals who loot, shoot and leave their hometowns awash in blood, bullets and broken glass. (Johnson, 1993, p. 31)[1]

With schools representing a microcosm of the community, standards of behavior within the community, or learned at home, are brought to school. Existing correlations between crime rates within the local community and the level of crimes within the school are clearly recognized by school administrators and teachers. Violence is expanding as an accepted way of resolving social conflict. Casual acceptance of physical means to solve problems between neighbors is replicated when arguments between students in the classroom become bloody. Rival feuds between adults in housing projects, the apartment building, or across farm fences are passed to younger family members, eventually spilling into the schools. Violent behavior of organized gangs is probably the most graphic example of community aggression with repercussions in schools. Tensions at home also spill into the school:

- Two middle school brothers reacted to their mother's drinking binges. One started fights and the other withdrew.
- Just before lunch an angry kindergartner hit his teacher with a chair. When we arrived at his home to talk with his mother, she opened the door, naked and stoned.
- Racial hatred taught and fostered at home may explode on a school bus. The 14-year-old nephew of a leader of a weekend warrior camp refused to release his choke hold on an African-American student on the bus one afternoon. In response to the bus driver's pleas to let go, he calmly replied, "I'm following orders, Sir." The boy's grandfather met the bus and driver the following morning with a .357 Magnum and a warning to never bother his grandson again.
- During the heyday of Cape Kennedy, increased numbers of student fights and outbursts precisely paralleled an impending launch. The same trends are evident during tough economic times in communities. Factory layoffs and strikes create tensions at home that are translated into angry retaliation in school.

- Victims of sexual aggression and humiliating behavior at home reenact such behavior in school on smaller or more vulnerable classmates.

Frustration, hurt, abuse, and fear arrive at school in many forms. Estimates of criminal behavior in schools include 204,000 incidents of aggravated assaults, 270,000 burglaries, 12,000 armed robberies, and 9,000 rapes annually (Rich, 1992). A lethal combination of factors accounts for the escalating violence within our culture and within our schools. To increase awareness of the complexities and interwoven nature of the major sources of violence, this chapter looks at the following key factors.

Key Factors to Consider

1. Dysfunctional families
2. Clashes of cultures and lack of community
3. Media messages
4. Prevalence of weapons
5. Denial, cover-up, and court systems
6. Drugs as big business
7. Gangs and other subculture activities
8. Catalytic events
9. Random violence

Dysfunctional Families

- Only 7% of families in 1985 had both working fathers and mothers supporting school-age children (Heath & McLoughlin, 1987).
- Percentages of children living with only their mothers doubled in the 1980s (Hofferth, 1987).
- Children from single-parent homes are twice as likely to drop out of school and more likely to be late, in trouble, and truant while enrolled in school (Eitzen, 1992).
- Eleven percent of newborns are drug exposed (O'Neil, 1991).

Soaring rates of teens giving birth, homeless families, and chemi-cally dependent parents contribute to the desperate plight of our children. Unemployment and underemployment escalate tension that fosters abuse, assault, and abandonment of children. Teenage mothers with no cultural background to read stories to their children or to even teach peek-a-boo cannot be expected to teach or model healthy ways of controlling anger. Violence of one family member toward another is an increasing problem, with physical and mental effects that extend to every member of the family (Lysted, 1986). From such unstable beginnings, children learn violent behavior that is then carried to school.

A second-wave effect of the absence of family structures includes children turning to cults, gangs, drugs, or crime for escape, recogni-tion, and identity. Because children under 18 will often go unconvicted or are easily paroled, they are used as perpetrators of crimes.

- A child in one elementary school was close to death after a boyfriend of her mother's forced an older sibling to kick the younger one for punishment. The child was placed in a foster home for 3 weeks and then released back to the mother and her boyfriend.
- Children's small size makes them ideal for use as "squeezes." Young children can be shoved into tiny openings in buildings to pass out stolen goods, or to let adults in through fire doors.
- For significant tips, youngsters are trained to become quite adept as lookouts for drug dealers and pimps.

Criminal activity is often the only opportunity that some young children have for success. They are rewarded and recognized; a pat-tern is learned. Aggressive criminal behavior is brought by some students to school each morning.

Clashes of Cultures and Lack of Community

Economic differences are the biggest cultural differences within our country. School communities within cities are commonly composed of new immigrants, mobile populations, and unemployed subcultures competing for jobs and the dignity that employment provides. Limited inexpensive housing, crowded conditions, opportunistic merchants, and unscrupulous employers add to the frustration. Continuous frustration will eventually erupt.

> Poverty itself does not generate violent behavior. It is the combination of poverty plus alienation, the hopeless feeling of despair in an uncaring nation, that is the seedbed of hostility, conflict, and violence. (Friedlander, 1993, p. 13)

Wandering populations include families living in cars or tents, as well as the homeless found under bridges and in abandoned buildings. Many families live in substandard housing or are crowded into apartments with other families. Physical solutions are often applied to problems of overcrowding.

- A first grader discussed his father's throwing his uncle through a sliding glass door the previous evening. "I think they will all move out today," was how he summarized the episode.
- On the first day of April, our school was suddenly inundated with new students. An apartment building had offered a month's free rent. Many families moved in and then out when the month was up and the evictions began.
- Following Hurricane Andrew in August 1992, schools in Orlando and other parts of Florida opened their doors for the new school year to dozens and even hundreds of new students from Miami. Many families who were renting a place to live simply got in their cars and moved north, leaving their few possessions to the winds. The high schools immediately experienced an epidemic of fighting as students attempted to release fear and frustration, and establish respect and new territory.
- In November, one of our seniors was selected as homecoming king. He also turned 18 that month. Because of the intense crowding from eight children in a newly combined family, his

stepfather threw him out of the house. He spent the rest of the
school year living in his car and, secretly, in our locker room.

The disenfranchised wander from city to city on rumors of jobs.
Bad luck or bad habits have produced situations where many of our
students do not know where home will be after school. A student
concluded that his family would be moving that night. His dad had
"run a car in from Alabama" the previous evening, and the police
would be after them now. The old Rodney Dangerfield joke about his
family moving and not telling him where they went is a tragic fear
and sometimes reality for some students.

There are no incentives for making friends. Continually moving
makes friendships painful. Survival skills and street smarts teach
them that it is safer to stay on the outside. They quickly learn to isolate
themselves and their feelings from others.

By the year 2020 the majority of most urban centers will be minorities, and half of the students in our schools will be members of various
minority groups. Orlando, Florida, provides a staggering example.
Students in Orlando's school district speak 56 languages and are from
174 countries (Orange County Public Schools, 1993). The district is
beset with the details and planning necessary to accommodate the
5,000 to 6,000 new students enrolling annually. To further entangle this
complex picture, many schools experience annual student turnover
rates above 80% (Hill, 1993).

The varieties of cultural differences are far beyond the number of
countries represented within a school district. Immigrants from each
country bring an assortment of standards of acceptable behavior. A
Hispanic mother was upset that her newly enrolled son was not
allowed to carry a knife to school. She explained her fear that he would
not be able to defend himself. A knife was considered essential for
defense in the New England high school he had previously attended.

The struggle of minority children to become successful is crystal-
lized in national dropout statistics. By age 25, 88% of white students
have completed high school, but only 60% of Hispanic students have
(Huelskamp, 1993). Diverse cultural values, efforts to find identity,
and difficult economic conditions contribute to clashes in the mixture
known as school.

Media Messages

- With unsupervised viewing, children annually experience 10,000 hours of television containing five to eight violent acts per hour (Bybee & Gee, 1982).
- Watching cartoons on Saturday morning will supply a child with 26.4 incidents of violence each hour (Eitzen, 1992).
- Before a child is 18, he or she has seen 100,000 beer commercials (Eitzen, 1992).

Increased cable accessibility spirals children's experience with sex, murder, torture, and aggressive, as well as degrading behavior toward women, minorities, and the less fortunate in society. Add to the television totals the hours spent in front of video games. The "Nintendo generation" receives strong messages concerning the use of violence to solve conflict.

Messages in movies, videos, advertising, song lyrics, and even on "900 numbers" smother children. The message that materialism, easy sex, drug use, and violence are glamorous saturates their senses during the years when value structures are forming.

Prevalence of Weapons

- Guns are brought to school each day in the United States by 135,000 students (Memphis City Schools, 1993).
- Memphis City Schools increased firearms suspensions by tenfold from 1983 until 1993 (Memphis City Schools, 1993).
- Twenty percent of students in a national survey expressed concern about guns in their schools. Thirty-one percent of their parents feared that their children would be injured in a gun-related incident at or on their way to school ("Thirty-One Percent of Parents," 1993).

As aggressive behavior increases throughout the community, numbers of aggressive incidents increase in schools. As weapons become more common within households, they more easily appear in schools.

Status in many communities is achieved by the weapon of choice, whether it is a box cutter or an automatic weapon. For some adolescents, manhood and womanhood are defined by the kind of gun they carry. One afternoon, customs officials from Miami called to ask about a student's enrollment status in our school. He had been arrested with three other juveniles stealing automatic weapons from a government armory. An active market waiting for the sale of automatic weapons within our school community had been temporarily thwarted.

Affluent suburbs and rural communities are not immune from escalating numbers and magnitudes of weapons. Fairfax County, Virginia, officials rarely dealt with incidents of guns in their schools before 1990. In the first months of the 1992-1993 school year, 50 of the 86 recommendations for expulsion dealt with weapon possessions (Lawton, 1993). In the 1991-1992 school year, Prince Georges County, Maryland, public schools experienced a 200% increase in student firearms possession. A statewide survey in Iowa found that 23% of the high school students carried a weapon to school (Landen, 1992).

Parents also bring guns to school. After a school play, a mother pulled a gun on another mother, to emphasize the threat that her paroled son would rape the other woman's kindergartner if she testified against her on a drug charge. When the principal saw the mother who had been making threats arrive on campus, she called the police and locked the kindergartner in her office. The mother was arrested as the encounter began.

Gun sales have increased in recent years to wider audiences, with soaring sales often responding to local outbreaks of violence. Guns purchased in response to fear are commonly kept at home, fully loaded. School security experts and police officers estimate that 80% of guns brought to school are brought from home (Harrington-Lueker, 1992a), and most students who are apprehended claim to be carrying guns for protection.

Just like the August advertising campaigns of WalMart and Penneys, one gun shop in California advertised a selected weapon as its "Back to School Special." Access to a weapon for most children is simple, and guns are increasingly powerful and more easily hidden. Disguised weapons are also publicly available. A gun shaped like a beeper is legally sold in many states.

Using a gun to calm one's fear or anger leads to tragedy. As Gaustad (1991) so clearly noted, "The presence of weapons, particularly guns, means that schoolyard conflicts that once ended in black eyes and bloody noses now sometimes end in death" (p. 6).

Denial, Cover-Up, and Court Systems

For every reported crime within schools, 58 remain unreported to the police (Quarles, 1989). Lack of consequence for committing crimes leads to more crimes. Crimes go unreported for a variety of reasons.

- Dealing with only the most severe cases is an issue of survival for some school administrators and justice systems. Sheer numbers make it impossible to process the paper, gather testimony, compile the case, appear in court, guarantee due process, and all the other complicated steps in working within the criminal justice system.

- In some schools and districts, administrators look the other way rather than address what is happening. If they so choose, principals can legitimately be consumed with paperwork and administrative details so they never see or talk with students. Principals' reality becomes their office. They lose touch with what students are experiencing. This phenomenon can become magnified for district office administrators.

- Occasionally, school officials view suppressing and ignoring criminal behavior as good public relations. In some areas, these tactics reflect pressure from real estate agencies. New customers and home values within a school district will diminish at the hint of unsafe schools.

- Schools within systems are often compared and treated competitively rather than cooperatively. This policy leads to pressure to control numbers, rather than effectively charting and analyzing patterns of behavior. An assistant principal recalled asking his principal if he could proceed with the suspension of a student who had a succession of assaults on other students. The principal pulled out his calculator to check his percentage of suspensions for the year to date. Finding the percentage below that of two rival high schools, he approved the suspension.

- Political pressure is often placed on principals to maintain low rates of violent behavior. When school boards or other political structures have extensive personnel power, important numbers for decision making and problem solving can become suppressed or distorted statistics. Realistic statistics could result in a principal's losing his or her job.
- Students and sometimes teachers fail to report crimes for fear of retribution. Intimidation and threats effectively subdue exposure.

Judicial intolerance of school violence is strongly emphasized in the Supreme Court's denouncement of school misbehavior in the *New Jersey v. T.L.O.* ruling (Shoop & Dunklee, 1992). A safe and orderly environment is expected and desired. Maintaining a consistently safe setting for students is complicated by the realities of excessive numbers of students and the amount of time students are in school settings. With before- and after-school programs, many students are in school 12 or 13 hours a day. Consider (a) the numbers and hours, (b) the pay schedules and reward systems of teachers and daycare workers, which do not necessarily secure or retain the best workers, and (c) the lack of reasonable ratios of adult personnel with students. The approach to supervision of student behavior becomes haphazard and risky.

Drugs as Big Business

Schools are an ideal center to gather future customers and workers in the massive business of illegal drugs. Highly organized groups and impulsive, desperate individuals are available marketers in nearly every high school in the country. The product and sales methods vary in intensity. Basic economics make the risk worth the potential profit.

The impact of drugs on our students is clear. Winters (1992) estimates that 85% to 95% of adolescents involved with the judicial system have drug problems. Drug involvement becomes inevitably linked to gang activity, organized crime, robbery, and assault.

No group is immune to the direct and indirect damage created by substance abuse; everyone is affected. Drug users sacrifice links to friends and families, often their careers, and, if left unchecked, their lives. The second wave of suffering involves the effect of usage on other family members who experience the pain, heartache, and sometimes terror of being associated with the user. Other members of society are victims of crimes committed by users to secure the money or power that evades them.

Links to violent behavior, in both direct and indirect ways, are more prevalent with some drugs of choice than others; and drugs affect different people in different ways. Crack users commonly exhibit a pattern of unpredictable and aggressive behavior. With no idea of the possible effects or reactions, teenagers will sometimes take a handful of whatever prescription medicine their group collects. Excessive alcohol levels can create a variety of personalities within the same individual. As with the use of weapons and initial gang membership, alcohol abuse is beginning at earlier and earlier ages. Winters (1992) points out that one third of children in rural areas have had their first drink by the age of 10. He further reminds us that "substance abuse among youth transcends geographical, racial, and socioeconomic boundaries" (p. 25). Substance abuse and its negative effects are covering a wider and wider territory.

Gangs and Other Subculture Activities

Gangs take a variety of forms: Many gangs within our cities are generational, with longstanding feuds, defined territory, chains of command, rituals and traditions; other gangs are newly and loosely forming as a subgroup attempts to carve an identity.

Two alarming trends of gang activity are evolving. Gangs were once an inner-city problem, but the suburbs are providing ripe new territory with more available money, broken families, and smaller groups of law enforcement (Moriarty & Fleming, 1990). Recently a rural Appalachian school experienced the growth of two gangs after a student from an urban gang moved to the area. Within 2 weeks of the student's arrival, there were red and blue bandannas prevalent throughout the campus and the community, identifying the gang affiliation.

The second trend involves younger and younger membership. Middle schools are now feeling the impact that was once largely confined to high schools. Even the Ku Klux Klan and other organized groups fostering hate crimes, such as neo-Nazis, skinheads, and Satanists, seek younger membership (Bodinger-de Uriarte, 1991).

Once a child becomes a gang member, the odds are overwhelming that he or she will never disassociate. Gangs provide status, safety, belonging, and opportunities for income to their members. Gang activity within schools creates intertwined problems with drug trafficking and related violent behavior. Territorial battles, recruiting needs, initiation demands, and access to weapons are other catalysts for violence. Territorial pride can justify the assault of a freshman in the wrong school hallway. Recruiting needs and initiation demands can be met by punching a teacher or raping a classmate. Easy access to weapons makes problem solving a matter of determining who has the most damaging gun.

Catalytic Events

Special events of a local or national nature sometime contain potential catalysts for violence. An annual football game with a rival provides the opportunity, increased emotion, or excuse for aggression to occur. Fights, emulating what occurs at professional sports events, can break out on the field or in the stands. The number of students and nonstudents at postgame rallies at fast-food restaurants can become massive. Problems starting there extend to school on Monday or lead to retaliation at another campus. Retaliation has accelerated from stringing trees with toilet paper or spray painting the school to drive-by shootings, gang rapes, and beatings.

One high school principal moved two annual football games with heated rivals to Saturday mornings. During Friday night games, peaceful fans and families learned to leave at halftime. By 9:00 p.m. older groups were sufficiently drunk and would arrive to fight. A Saturday morning schedule defused the crowds, transforming the former combat zone into a collegiate atmosphere. The troublemakers were still at home, hung over.

A musical act, multicultural celebration, or contest can be the reason for bad feelings to explode. In one area, the annual state fair has become a demolition derby between gangs with reputations on the line. In recent years, gang fistfights have advanced to include drive-by shootings.

Events from larger arenas can have negative local effects. The 1992 Rodney King verdict caused not only mayhem in Los Angeles but also reasons elsewhere in the country to bring weapons to school or excuses to have shorter fuses in daily school life. Ku Klux Klan rallies in one city can lead to tensions in other neighborhoods. Violent activities from other settings spill into the school, catching innocent bystanders in the cross fire.

Random Violence

Random selection of a school as a center for aggression is the most perplexing violent situation to be considered. Since 1984, 30 documented accounts have been made in which an unbalanced person entered a school with a weapon. Deaths of children are usually the startling outcome of intruder violence.

Intruders committing violent acts in schools fall into two categories. The first type of intruder is a marginal member of the school community. This person may be an estranged spouse of a staff member, the noncustodial parent of a student, a disgruntled former employee, or an angry parent.

Unlike crime in other settings, the majority of perpetrators in schools fall into the second category, as complete strangers to the victims. The predator may never have entered the school before and may have no association with the school. The school is randomly selected. Violence from perpetrators is most difficult to manage proactively because of the arbitrary nature of the crime.

Many random criminals either need power or disdain authority. Schools symbolize authority that once held power over them and represent a setting in which they were unsuccessful, bullied, or humiliated. Full of easy victims for the criminal, schools offer a perfect target for random violence for several reasons:

- Schools have heavy concentrations of people.
- School employees are generally trusting, helpful, and open people.
- Elementary schools, especially, have many defenseless children and often no adult males.

- Dedicated teachers are often found in isolated areas of the campus, after hours or on weekends, preparing their classrooms or planning lessons.
- Schools are commonly wide open to the public.
- Schools have many doors, with access in several directions.
- Campuses are often expansive, with many square feet of hallways.
- Schools are full of nooks and crannies.
- Landscaping around buildings is often advantageous to concealment.
- Security guards and systems are reserved for evenings, or only for schools in "tough" neighborhoods.

Anticipation and careful planning can reduce the probability of damage occurring within any school or district.

Final Thoughts

According to the 1994 report from the Children's Defense Fund, the number of children killed by guns from 1979 through 1991 exceeded the number of American soldiers lost in the Vietnam war. Violence is prevalent and pervasive in our culture. Creating safe schools begins with principals who are willing to address the problem before tragedy strikes.

An awareness of the main sources of violence assists principals and district leaders in identifying signals of possible violence. Comprehensive planning to handle emergencies is critical. Meeting the needs of students seeking identity, handling minor situations before they magnify, and creating a sense of community in the school can assist in reducing the probability of violent behavior. A variety of alternatives appear in the chapters ahead.

Note

1. Reprinted courtesy of SPORTS ILLUSTRATED from Volume 79, Issue 1 (1993). Copyright © 1993, Time Inc. "The Agony of Victory" by W. O. Johnson. All Rights Reserved.

Violence in Schools

Not Just an Urban Issue

V iolence is *not* just . . .

- an urban issue
- a high school problem
- the principal's responsibility

Approaches to maintaining safe and orderly environments for students require complex, comprehensive planning and commitment. The ideal climate for learning cannot be established by a lone leader within a building. Good schools, safe schools require wide community care and dedication. The chapters in this book address possibilities for making schools safe.

Throughout the country schools have found successful approaches, used innovative strategies, and perfected techniques to provide a safe and stimulating setting for students. The most effective combination

15

for your school or district requires collaborative planning to extract the bits and pieces to fit your unique needs.

A few fundamentals are universal when creating and maintaining safe schools. If your school is just like it was when you and your grandparents were in school, your school is probably behind. Lack of fit exists between an 1880s model for schooling and the needs of students who will live their lives in the 2000s. Schools still run on calendars convenient for shipbuilding and harvesting. Schools are in session during hours fitting 1950 television families like the Cleavers and Nelsons, where Mom stayed home and Dad was a white-collar breadwinner.

Symptoms of the misfit include dismal stories full of low standardized test scores, excessive dropout rates, and illiterate graduates in a high-tech world. The structure of many school systems is not working for today's students.

The expression of violence in our schools serves as the warning that change must occur. Responsibility for creating a climate for change rests with our educational leaders within each school, as well as in central offices, state departments, and legislative chambers. Priorities have been redefined. To deal effectively with the essential issue of curbing violence within our schools, we must apply our broad understandings of the surrounding issues contributing to school aggression.

Establishing School Wellness

During the 1980s schools with good things happening for students were put under a microscope. Researchers attempted to determine the factors that created the most effective schools for student learning. Solid information was contributed about elements in schools where learning takes place and students are successful contributors. A consistent finding in studies of school effectiveness was that a "safe and orderly" environment was paramount for learning to take place (Purkey & Smith, 1982).

A single act of violence within a school has the potential to destroy any possibility of a safe and orderly environment. It deters the fundamental purpose of schools. Just as our personal wellness depends

---

BOX 2.1

Negative School Climates Lack . . .

Spirit	Pride
Ownership	Discipline
Care and Tending	Esprit de Corps
Community Ties	Parental Input

---

on constant maintenance of many aspects of our lives, making our schools safe also requires consistent orchestration of a complicated set of interwoven factors. And just as our wellness is largely a personal responsibility, school wellness begins within each building. Certain basic characteristics are required. Essentials for school wellness include the following:

- A sense of community must be created.
- Care and consideration must be extended to each person within the school environment.
- Substantive activities must be occurring within each classroom.
- School facilities must be maintained and tended.
- Parental and neighborhood ties must be developed.

Although many factors are essential for all schools, unique prescriptions for creating and maintaining a safe school are required in each setting. Schools as microcosms of their communities have different needs and strengths.

Forms of School Violence

Violence in schools takes two major forms. First, violence can pervade the climate of schools, allowing negative events to escalate into increasingly damaging patterns. See Box 2.2 for an outline of this.

Examples of this downward spiral exist in cities and towns throughout the country. The speed of spiraling decay is linked to economic

---

BOX 2.2

Spiraling Opportunities for Violence

Negative Climate

A Catalytic Incident

   A group of students intimidate other students.

Escalating Results

   Enrollment declines.

   1. Financially able parents move their children to private schools.
   2. Mobile people move from the neighborhood as real estate values decline.
   3. Student and staff absenteeism increases.
   4. Some students dropout rather than live with fear.

   Academic performance and morale decline.

   1. Many good teachers leave.
   2. Competent staff become hardened.
   3. Expectations of staff for student performance drop.
   4. Job performance becomes minimal, with survival-level behavior.

   Public support declines.

   1. Incentive to financially support the school drops.
   2. Other resources pull their support.
   3. Media and public voice disgust.

---

factors. Intervention reversing the trend is possible at any point along the way; but as with many dysfunctional factors, intervention is less complex at the beginning of decline than after years of depravation.

The *second* form of violence involves random mayhem, with the school as its setting. Ironically, individuals can eat right and exercise regularly and still get hit by lightning. Schools are as vulnerable. Fine schools with exemplary learning taking place can be sites of random violence: Students can be taken hostage by a deranged escapee; a disgruntled bus driver can open fire from the roof; a drug dealer can seek revenge with an automatic weapon in a school hallway. This random violence is often impossible to anticipate. But immediate and long-term damage can be reduced with proactive leadership and planning.

Leadership is the key factor in combating both escalating and random forms of school violence. For sustaining a safe and orderly environment, a combination of leadership at the district and school level is essential.

- The district office holds many responsibilities for support and service to individual schools. The selection of each school's leader may be the most critical decision in stemming school violence.
- Within each school, leadership cannot be concentrated or horded by one individual. Policies and behaviors of effective principals will foster and mentor leadership within others to create a climate in which violent behavior finds no way to germinate.

Scenarios to Consider

School wellness depends on daily maintenance of essential factors, leading to a positive, healthy school climate and development of plans to reduce the damage caused by random factors. Observing from outside can often help us review our own setting with new eyes. Three scenarios follow to be used to:

1. Identify the effective leadership behavior in place.
2. List factors and actions necessary in each setting to reduce the possibility of violence.
3. Finally, compile a list of strategies that should have been previously established to assist in maintaining the safety of students.

Scenario 1: Poinciana High School

American's secondary schools are often the center for violent acts of young people toward one another. Each month about 28,200 students are attacked in our nation's secondary schools (Greenbaum &

Turner, 1989). School leadership is pivotal in creating an environment in which students are safe. Consider Carmen Hernandez's options.

Poinciana High School is visible from I-95. Thousands of people pass it each day. Many are on their way north into Miami to work; others, southbound, are passing through for a few days of escapism in the Florida Keys. Poinciana High School is about 12 years old. The concrete block buildings are continually assaulted by the relentless sun, adolescent expression, and time. Hurricane Andrew sandblasted the walls and removed the roof. Repairs have been made, but the landscape still attests to the parching effect of the wind.

Neighborhoods surrounding Poinciana High are connections of housing developments. Baby boomers' first or second purchases are rapidly being sold to first-generation immigrants hoping for different opportunities. The less-expensive housing developments are gradually becoming rental units. Some rentals house two or three families. The lucrative career of drug dealing attracts both out-of-town traffic and law enforcement attention to two apartment buildings and one street in particular.

Unrest between two subcultures spawned in the community festers in Poinciana High School. First-generation Puerto Ricans are angry at New York Puerto Ricans moving into the community. The Mi-Rican gang is known as the Bu Boys because their central hangout is in an abandoned electronics store on Malibu Drive. New Ricans, Puerto Ricans who immigrated through New York, were more recently organized. They can be identified throughout campus by the professional football leather jackets they wear.

In these past few days before spring break, Carmen Hernandez has felt growing tensions: Discipline referrals are up, and three fights broke out today in the breezeway where sophomores eat lunch.

Yesterday, during a suspension hearing, she was verbally attacked. The barrage of words held the usual frustration, anger, and resentment, but for the first time she encountered personal ethnic attacks. Carmen was promoted to principal from an assistant principalship in Poinciana 7 years ago. Her heritage had been a source of pride for the minority Cuban population within the school and neighborhood. Over the past few years, the 32% Cuban population diminished to 10%, although Spanish is the first language of 43% of the school population. Cambodian and Vietnamese students account for 8% of the student body, with another 7% of the students being African American.

While she was in the midst of reviewing discipline referrals, Mr. Hunter, one of her assistant principals, entered her office with Officer Grant. He was there to inform her that an extensive drug bust had just taken place in the Palms Apartments. More than 50 arrests were made, including three of her students. One of her students was shot and killed in the gunfire.

Considerations

1. What other immediate information does Carmen need?
2. What actions need to be taken within the next 24 hours?
3. What existing leadership qualities do you see that are beneficial to this school environment?
4. What long-range plans should be put into effect?

Scenario 2: Morgan Middle School

Lasting patterns of problem solving are developed by students during their middle school or junior high school years. Unfortunately, when a problem exists, physical retaliation is the choice of too many students. Junior high or middle school rates of assault and robberies are twice as high as high school rates (Toby, 1983). Consider what could be done at Morgan Middle School to turn around the negative undercurrent that suddenly becomes too obvious to deny.

For years Milford School District's biggest problem was deciding how to manage a diminishing student population. Then, with the influence of a local alumnus turned senator, the town's small teachers' college became a university. Within the past 3 years, a medical school was added and a large medical supply company relocated to Milford. Construction companies were prospering as they scrambled to build office space for several new medical and technology businesses. Milford was suddenly experiencing development of a bevy of fastfood restaurants, an expanded mall, several small service industries, followed by a housing shortage.

The heart attack of a school board member created a need for a recent election that changed local political history. Bob Fawcett, one of the "new group," joined four board members who were local residents with generational ties to Milford. Defeating several opponents, Bob's campaign targeted problems at Morgan Middle School.

Built 20 years ago, Morgan Middle School occupies a pleasant hill next to Lion's Club Park in the middle of town. The facility did not contain the 800 students for which it was built until 5 years ago. Now 1,100 students bump through its halls. Based on an estimation from the seven feeder elementary schools, the student population could fall just short of 1,200 next year. As principal for 2 years, Leslie Reeves has seen administrative time consumed with hiring new teachers and finding space.

Mr. Fawcett's campaign and subsequent election had become an embarrassment to Morgan Middle. His campaign highlighted growing rumors from Morgan, concerning charges of drug problems, intimidation, extortion, and assault on students by other students. Students' statements were put in campaign ads and played out by the local media.

Leslie felt that everything was being distorted. A few fights were normal for any school. Morgan's dropout rate was growing, but some students could not be reliably tracked with all of the recent change. The publicity seemed unjustified and unwarranted until this morning, when Leslie walked into a school bathroom and found a student in a toilet stall suffering from a severe stab wound.

Considerations

1. What short-term and long-term actions need to take place?

2. What factors produce blinders for leadership?

Scenario 3: Prairie View Elementary School

Headlines and stories about violence are commonly set in urban schools, and research has also emphasized the aggression in city schools. A false sense of security pervades many rural and suburban schools, but there is no immunity to violence for any setting.

Nor are elementary schools more immune to violence than secondary schools. In fact, for several reasons they may be more vulnerable. Consider what you would do if you were principal of Prairie View Elementary School.

8:00 a.m. Chilling January winds were blowing over the Wyoming fields behind the school as Matt Evans helped the driver of the special education bus unload her five students. Because of the 83-mile route, the two youngest were usually asleep when they arrived at Prairie View Elementary School. Three other buses had already deposited their 97 students. The 11 students who walked from the small Prairie View community had already found their classrooms.

Matt, the school principal, saw Nancy Stealey pull into the parking lot as the last bus left. She was 35 minutes late, and her third-grade students would be noisily playing in the classroom. Nancy had been late several times within the past 2 weeks. Matt had casually mentioned the problem to her, but now a more definitive conversation would need to follow.

Another busy day was beginning for Matt Evans. A leaky water heater, the custodian out with the flu, and heating problems in one classroom would demand attention. After weeks of careful planning by all seven teachers, a reading celebration involving almost three dozen parents and community members was scheduled for 10:00 a.m.

Matt stopped by the office to be brought up-to-date by Mrs. Burns, the school secretary. After 13 years, Mrs. Burns knew everyone in the tiny Prairie View community. She exemplified the finest of school secretaries. In one sentence, she conveyed that everything was under control. Nothing urgent was waiting in the usual phone messages and school district mail. He could survey the classrooms to see that instruction was beginning smoothly.

His first stop was Nancy Stealey's room. Students were in their seats. A half dozen children were reading books, but the rest were talking. Mrs. Stealey was nowhere to be seen. Matt quieted the room and began a discussion concerning the reading they would share with their special guests later that morning. Nancy Stealey hurried into the room, visibly embarrassed when she saw Matt.

10:00 a.m. As he proceeded to the second grade, he found their classroom much too cold and moved them into the library. His last stop, at the kitchen, found a crew of three men removing the water heater. Mrs. McCoy, the cafeteria manager, was anxious about the prospect of no hot water, with lunch beginning in a little more than an hour. Discussion with the work crew, concerning help with the heating repairs in the second grade, was interrupted by an odd-sounding Mrs. Burns on the public address system. She was paging Matt to call the office, and he moved quickly to the kitchen phone. Later he remembered that his uneasiness at her urgency was well founded.

In a voice she forced to remain calm, Mrs. Burns told Matt that a stranger was in the school. She had seen a man enter the front door and hurry past the office. When she approached and asked to help him, he pushed her against the wall and kept walking. He was dirty, staring oddly, and carrying a small suitcase.

Considerations

1. As principal of the school, what would your next moves be?
2. What advantages do you have in this situation?
3. What disadvantages do you have?
4. What procedures should be in place to assist in situations such as this?
5. What leadership qualities does Matt possess that are conducive to reducing the potential of violence at Prairie View Elementary School?
6. What characteristics of elementary schools make them more vulnerable to random violence than most secondary schools?

Final Thoughts

What occurred at Prairie View, Poinciana, and Morgan could happen anywhere. The circumstances in these three schools can be useful to school administrators in considering suitable strategies for each situation. Transferring similar circumstances to local school settings can make it easier to develop plans to effectively prevent or prepare for violent encounters. Strategies and programs throughout the following chapters could be applied to produce safer climates at Poinciana, Morgan, and Prairie View.

Groups of principals or teams within the school can use these scenarios, or ones specifically tailored to their demographics, for discussion. Planning sessions should follow, in which schoolwide and districtwide approaches to reducing possibilities for violence or minimizing the potential damage of a violent incident are designed.

Leadership and Teaching Strategies to Create Safe Schools

In a small middle school in Tennessee, a fight broke out during lunch. A food service director was standing in the hall as students were being dispersed. A student, impressed with the discord, stopped and excitedly asked her what she thought about the fight. She replied that she felt that students should get along. The student looked at her in disgust and said, "That only happens in dreams, and dreams don't happen here."

What must happen in schools so dreams do happen? Harrington-Lueker (1992a) advocated that "until individual schools establish a strong enough cultural identity of their own, the street culture will continue to rule school corridors" (p. 26). From your experience as a principal and from success stories that you have heard, we know that in most cases the school has the power to overcome even negative home settings. Garbarino, Dubrow, Kostelny, and Pardo (1992) felt that "the vast majority of poor children, even poor children from chaotic families, are not psychologically ill and can perform adequately in school, provided the school climate is positive" (p. 168). *The principal within the school is the central factor in establishing a positive cultural identity or school climate.*

When people write about organizations, the word *climate* is often used. Climate is difficult to define and measure because the term refers to an invisible feeling that is encountered. School climate is apparent when you walk onto a school campus and into the building. School climates range from pleasant settings, where learning is the central focus, to chaotic institutions, with loose bands of students creating the standards of behavior.

Quick Indicators of Positive School Climate

- Smiles on the faces of students and staff
- Clean and well-tended facilities
- A warm welcome
- Teachers, principal, and staff interacting with students, not located behind desks as barriers
- Visible evidences of learning
- Students behaving courteously to one another
- Clearly posted directions and informed encounters

Climate affects whether anger, aggression, and violent behaviors flourish or fade. School leadership is the pivotal determiner of school climate. The studies of effective schools identified the relationship between students' chances for academic success and a climate that is collegial and collaborative, and fosters a sense of community. Barth (1990), in describing a school as a community of learners, pictures a school where:

teachers and principals talk with one another about practice, observe one another engaged in daily activities, share their knowledge of their craft with one another, and actively help one another become more skillful. In a collegial school adults and students are constantly learning because everyone is a staff developer for everyone else. (p. 513)

The principal determines whether a sense of community is formed.

Dimensions of Leadership

Principals as primary school leaders face an increasingly complex task. The dimensions of the job have changed and expanded with new roles and responsibilities for schools. Leadership and the principalship have been closely examined in recent years.

Leadership is recognized as a composition of dimensions, including such ethereal qualities as sensitivity, flexibility, and intuitive skill. Being able to lead in contemporary schools requires a high degree of competence. Principals must be dynamic combinations of entrepreneur and risk taker while simultaneously empowering others. Effective leaders are described as capable of achieving attention through vision, meaning through communication, trust through positioning, and finally, a willingness to self-deploy and empower others (Bennis & Nanus, 1985). The lone warrior and the benevolent dictator are ineffective leaders in today's society, and those anachronistic examples who remain in the schools are rapidly becoming extinct.

Leadership and Teaching Strategies
for Reducing the Potential for Violence

The school principal is a constant model of the level of expected behavior within the school. Many practices of effective principals directly and indirectly discourage behaviors that could bring harm to members of the school community. Principals can reduce violence through interwoven behaviors and techniques:

1. The principal must be highly visible.
2. Expectations for attendance must be understood, and require effort to be attained.

3. Instructional leadership must support a curriculum that creates successful students.

4. Time on task must be maximized.

5. Leadership must be shared.

6. Communication with the external and internal community is multidimensional.

7. Competent staff must be found and supported.

8. Parents and the community must be involved in school activities.

9. School operations must be localized to meet community needs.

The Principal Must Be Highly Visible

The principal should be ubiquitous. When the principal is highly visible, reduction in school violence occurs. Effective principals are found checking whether broken glass was cleaned up around the refuse bins. They can be found serving on the cafeteria line, in and out of classrooms, in the middle of the athletic field, in the stands observing band practice, examining a roof under repair, picking up a stray piece of paper in a hallway. There is no routine pattern. Such activities model that school leadership cares about the quality of performance of every individual within the school.

Within the community, the principal can be found at the farthest bus stop talking with parents before daylight, in apartment recreation rooms for a question-and-answer session, in the parking lot as students arrive, and in managers' offices of local businesses, gathering support for a school partnership.

As a new assistant principal, one of my first assignments from the principal was to ride the bus routes. It took weeks to cover them all. Waiting at the bus stop one morning for the buses to pick up three loads of children from one trailer park, I understood why I dealt with so many bus referrals from this one spot. After I rode sandy trails through orange groves and cornfields to migrant shacks, I understood when a mother told me she did not have time to talk with her son. He was the middle one of nine children. She worked in the cornfields from daylight to dark, fed the baby, and fell asleep.

As a principal, I continued the practice. On morning routes I saw students leave tents to catch the bus and I understood the uncombed hair. On hot Florida afternoons, experiencing the 30-mile route into the boggy area south of the international airport, I knew why the students were tired when they reached home.

Expectations for Attendance Must Be
Understood and Require Effort to Be Attained

Principals in high achieving schools place great emphasis on high achievement (Bossert, Dwyer, Rowan, & Lee, 1982). Performance standards for student behavior and academic work are clearly defined and understood. High expectations regarding student attendance are also critical. Students not in school are not progressing academically. Poor attendance must be a warning for school officials to take active measures to curtail the pattern.

Students not attending school are often in trouble: Some children are babysitting siblings under unsuitable conditions; others are covering their parents' responsibilities in other ways. While visiting a bus stop where many students waited before dark, I learned that a fourth grader was missing school to guard boxes. The mother and three children had been evicted, their possessions thrown in the street. The student had been assigned the task of sitting on the boxes while her mother was at work. Two men, next-door neighbors who were rumored to be drug dealers, had stolen their food stamps from the boxes the previous day.

Instead of being in school, older students are sometimes tied into neighborhood theft, or are using school hours to be sexually active. Many young children kept home during the day are being sexually abused while other members of the household are gone. An elementary student missed 2 of her 5 years in school because she was kept at home by an abusive grandfather. Years later, when the pattern was beginning again with the girl's own daughter, she finally let a family service agency intervene. Poor attendance signals a need for quick intervention.

Instructional Leadership Supports
Curriculum That Creates Successful Students

The principal must demonstrate, through direct and indirect action, that he or she has a passion for learning. "Head learner" is the term Barth (1990) used to refer to the function of leading the instruction within the school. The principal should find joy and renewal being with students and visiting classrooms.

Due to the complex nature of learning, the principal looks for underlying correlations and combinations that produce success for students. Good instructional leaders find a delicate balance between being nurturing yet disturbing to the status quo (Northern & Bailey, 1991). Teachers and staff are supported while finding better ways of assisting students. The principal works with teachers to seek answers to learning problems.

Student success is primary to the school culture. When learning is taking place in the type of climate established by true instructional leaders, violence and aggression find, at best, slippery footholds. Students successfully moving toward attainable, challenging, and visible learning goals are too involved in seeking their future to participate in violence and aggression.

Instructional leaders foster quality learning. Indicators that quality learning is taking place include the following:

- Responsibility for learning and working hard rests with the student. School staff are present to facilitate, and to sometimes structure, the sequence.
- Students are active in their work, solving problems.
- Students want to know answers to questions they have considered.
- Students are using written and oral language to learn. Small groups of students talk about solutions.
- Assessment of learning begins with the students' self-examination. Assessment is "a means of facilitating learning" (Glatthorn, 1992, p. 119).
- Students are learning content that matters.

Similarities to Glatthorn's indicators can be found in research related specifically to improving academic performance in tough schools. After 15,000 hours of study in inner-city schools, Rutter, Maughan, Mortimer, Ouston, and Smith (1979) located academic measures that related to desirable school outcomes. Better student behavior and attendance are related to several specific teacher practices that include:

- displaying student work
- assigning students to tasks requiring library use
- assigning homework and giving feedback on it
- emphasizing reward rather than punishment

Other techniques that improve academic performance include:

- maintaining an academic focus with the whole class and individuals
- facilitating discussion and assignments so each person responds and participates
- allocating time for repeated success and reinforcement
- providing time to establish, review, and reinforce desirable behavior
- moving among students to provide individual assistance and encouragement
- conveying warmth simultaneously with an atmosphere of task orientation

Success leads to attempts to be successful again. Students who like school have high self-esteem when they are learning and can see that they are progressing. Students can identify the progress they are making. Improved student behavior is directly tied to expectations regarding achievement.

Time on Task Must Be Maximized

A variety of factors determines how much time is spent on meaningful instruction within a school day (see Box 3.1). Sufficient instructional time is prerequisite to enhancing the quality of instruction.

BOX 3.1

Factors That Affect Learning Time

Student Factors

Personal Behavior	Psychological Traits	
misbehavior	aptitude	prior knowledge
absenteeism	ability	motivation
tardiness		

Teacher Factors

Personal Skills	Teaching Strategies	
managerial skills	whole or small group	problem solving
preparation	behavior management	approaches
organizational ability	cooperative learning	seatwork as busy work
planning	evaluation techniques	peer tutoring
goal setting		

Indirectly, the principal can support students and teachers in increasing their instructional time. For instance, programs supporting positive attendance and rewarding student punctuality are moves in the right direction. Attendance incentive programs start with analysis of attendance data. Breakfast for perfect attendance, local media support, calls to parents of every student absent, and home visits have produced positive results. One such effort in a district in South Carolina moved student attendance rates from 89th to 27th in the state (Woodall & Bond, 1993).

Opportunities for teachers to learn, observe, and share effective classroom procedural and instructional techniques create awareness of student time on task. Maximizing teachers' instructional time by circumventing interruptions, menial tasks, and outside interference falls within the direct responsibility of the principal. Increasing instructional time is possible through a variety of policies, as well as professional development activities.

Establish a Procedure About Use of the Intercom. A loose-leaf notebook can be placed by the intercom, and all announcements for the day are logged into the page and are made once. There is a common joke within many schools about "frustrated disc jockeys" on staff who love to hear themselves on the intercom. Staff laughter can often be heard when such a person begins an announcement. The situation loses its humor, however, when teachers talk about the vital point of a lesson that was interrupted, or the momentum of a small-group activity that was lost, when 2,000 students and staff stopped to hear about an after-school meeting affecting 10 students.

Technology eliminates much of this problem when each teacher has a monitor with bulletin board and voice mail software, so that all personnel are kept aware of activities. Commonly and effectively, morning announcements are conducted by students via classroom television. This can personalize the school climate, with lunch menus, birthdays, and other such announcements being covered, while establishing a quick pace to begin the day.

Supply and Assist Teachers in Making Better Use of Teachers' Aides and Volunteers. Teachers will gain further instructional time if they are supplied with as much assistance as possible to eliminate clerical and routine tasks. Unfortunately, teachers who are given assistants often are untrained in techniques to best utilize this help. This is another occasion in which collaborative groups of teachers can share proven practices for better utilizing the assistance they receive.

When the principal portrays classroom time as valuable, others regard it as such. Assuring more instructional time for teachers is the first step in creating an environment that continually seeks to enhance the quality of instruction.

Leadership Must Be Shared

Another shift in school leadership perspective reviews the ownership of leading. The school principal possesses the ability to extend leadership to others in the school setting. Competent, secure principals know that leadership should be fostered in all members of the school community.

Distribution of leadership occurs in two ways. Distribution is consciously shared or, in some states, legislated. Site-based councils of representative decision makers are established. Site-based teams commonly make implementation decisions regarding personnel, budget, and curriculum.

The second way that leadership is distributed is indirect. Leadership becomes possible in a climate of sharing, cooperation, and community. Teacher leadership must be encouraged. Barriers creating traditional classroom isolationism should be removed so that teachers will begin working, planning, teaching, and problem solving together. Barth (1990) noted that the teacher/principal relationship is indicative of all other relationships within the school. If the principal and teachers view each other in an adversarial, distrustful way, relationships with students will suffer. As feelings contributing to the overall climate deteriorate, the negative forces leading to aggression, violence, and harassment flourish.

Many school systems have structured programs to foster teacher leadership (Hill & Simmons, 1993). Teacher leader programs contain opportunities for:

- self-assessment of leadership potential
- examination of effective teaching
- studying change and improvement processes
- team-building training
- vision development
- understanding the power and political structure of the district and community
- reflection about practice

Professional development naturally occurs through teacher leader programs. After participating in teacher leader programs, teachers are more likely to improve their practice and work on curriculum development within the school. They begin viewing the school and district more globally.

Another benefit occurs from participatory leadership. When the principal models collaboration, participatory classrooms with class councils begin to emerge. Students who actively participate in decision making within the classroom, such as by establishing the rules and consequences for behavior, are less likely to behave violently.

In a report to Congress, the National Institute of Education (1978) found less violence in school settings in which students had opportunities for participating in the development of rules. When rules are considered fair and are perceived as fairly enforced, there is less frustration, desire for retaliation, and reason for aggressive behavior.

When class councils are coupled with curriculum that is purposefully designed to offer choices to students concerning their assignments and assessment, leadership will be further developed and distributed to students. At Brennan Middle School in Attleboro, Massachusetts, a town council model of subcommittees was used to determine class activities. Students developed critical thinking and problem-solving skills within their committees. Each day committees reported progress toward determined goals and received input from classmates (Blythe & Bradbury, 1993). Students gathered an increased sense of responsibility about the school as somewhere they belonged and wanted to be, rather than a place where they had to go.

Communication With the External and Internal Community Is Multidimensional

Grapevines. To maintain realistic perspectives, the principal must be hooked into community and school grapevines. Reliable sources are identified to give clear readings to the principal concerning reactions, events, and local temperature and tempo. Specific information forecasting violent behavior is often forwarded if lines of communication are available. Detroit Public Schools' Superintendent Jefferson relied on the importance of linkages to students for detecting weapons (Butterfield & Turner, 1989).

Opportunities must be structured to listen and establish dialogue with students. Scheduled and random opportunities must be available for principals to hear the concerns and hopes of students.

Reading and Sending Nonverbal Messages. A skillful principal reads each audience that is encountered. The principal's physical posture defines assurance and positive confidence. Energy and enthusiasm are easily recognized. Differences in nonverbal messages from diverse cultures are well understood. An effective principal knows what physical presence will be interpreted as supportive, aggressive, or harassing.

Using Technology and Other Communication Linkages. Efforts to communicate have to be relentless. Verbal, nonverbal, and print messages are all part of the campaign. Available technologies go further in assisting clear communication that is instantaneous. A computer on each teacher's desk can link teachers to each other, the principal to each teacher, and the teacher to the principal. These linkages reduce possibilities of inaccurate information, stifle rumors, speed assurances, and lead to problem solving.

Disruptions in the classroom can be relayed immediately. Support or help is available in minutes. When a student is sent to the office, problems can arise. Many problems with violence occur when a student leaves the classroom and then avoids the office. He or she goes to another room to gather a friend, heads to the parking lot or locker for a weapon, or generally roams around campus to let other students know that trouble occurred. This causes disturbances elsewhere. Instant communication allows the teacher to call for an escort if it is necessary.

Having some type of technology will allow teachers to be informed of emergency situations or the status of problem situations immediately and confidentially. Teachers with at least telephones in their classrooms report that their instructional time is saved by being able to immediately reach the front office. Telephones in classrooms also increase the probability of linking the teacher to parents on a more frequent basis.

Competent Teachers and Staff Must Be Found and Supported

Faculty at any school would ideally be a blend of people representing diverse backgrounds and regions, combined with graduates from the community being served by the school. A mixture of diverse and local faculty not only supports stronger curricular possibilities but also provides students with a range of successful role models.

Teams of faculty and staff members should participate in hiring processes. I found that when staff participated, they worked hard to orient the new person and assure him or her of success. When hiring teams selected candidates that were not my first choice, time proved that the group decisions were wise ones.

Care taken in selecting support staff should be as judicious as steps taken to hire teachers for the school. Custodians, teaching assistants, cafeteria workers, and office workers are critical to enhancing or harming school climate. They also demonstrate a work ethic and a variety of job opportunities to students who often lack many adult examples in their environment.

An essential member of our school staff had been a former semipro athlete. He completed one year of college and spent several years trying to become a major league ball player. He arrived with great dedication to the young people in his community and held high credibility with them. His style enabled him to defuse many volatile situations. Concomitantly he served as a positive male image for students in a community largely composed of single-parent house-holds.

Faculty should be encouraged to plan together, share common professional goals, and create a vision for learning within the school. Collegial pairs and cross-disciplinary teams are structures for establishing a setting of collaboration among teachers.

Employees who are committed to their profession, feel that they control their future directions, and accept changes are said to be hardy (Pines, 1980). Hardy persons will be more successful in their jobs while simultaneously remaining healthier than their less hardy counterparts.

Hardy teachers would assist students to be hardier individuals by their example and by their treatment of students. Hardy teachers would:

- give students choices in assignments and assessment
- find ways for students to be successful decision makers
- assist them in forming goals and planning strategies to achieve those goals

Hardy students view themselves as a positive part of the future. When this outlook is held, aggression and violence are unnecessary.

Teachers who lack a hardy personality are more likely to be reactive rather than proactive. They will be more authoritarian, inconsistent, and arbitrary in their approach to students. Aggressive, hostile teachers, who shout and handle students physically, create settings for students to react the same way (Research Action Brief, 1981). Ideally, schools should hire individuals who exhibit hardy behavior. Further, school leadership must provide both a school climate and professional development to assist teachers in becoming hardier. Increasing their opportunity to participate in decision making within the school is just one way to increase the teachers' commitment, feelings of internal locus of control, and ability to adapt to change.

Parents and the Community Must Be Involved in School Activities

Common sense and solid research make it obvious: Parents need to be involved in our schools. Following a review of 50 studies, Henderson (1987) found that students perform better in schools with strong parent involvement. Children from less fortunate families benefit the most when parents visit schools and take a role in learning. As attitudes about the value of schooling change at home, children begin to make true progress.

Parents with no transportation and those who do not speak English can still be part of learning. Teachers at McCoy Elementary School in Orlando, Florida, send home patterns and paper for parents to construct games for classrooms. In this community, many Hispanic mothers, otherwise isolated, can contribute to their children's classroom. A third grader proudly related that she had taught her mother some English by using classroom reading games at home.

Schools can send home projects for the family to produce together. For instance, kindergarten teachers at McCoy send home large patterns of a pumpkin in October and a turkey in November for each family to decorate as they wished. Finished products are hung in the halls and cafeteria, labeled with each family's name. The school also has a grant-funded Parent Resource Center. The center provides easy checkout of books and videos on parenting. The school guidance counselor volunteers free parenting classes, and other special funding makes family counseling available within the school in the evenings.

Teachers already highly successful in working with parents soon identify the rewards. Before school opens, some visit each child who will be in their classrooms. To convey that they are looking forward to seeing them on the first day, many teachers traditionally send children a letter. Providing extra funds for their time, or at least mileage, supports and recognizes the contribution of teachers willing to make home visits.

Many teachers, especially new teachers, are uncomfortable and reluctant to attempt contact with parents. Specific training is needed for teachers in techniques for conferencing with and involving parents. Setting realistic goals for this sometimes new dimension helps assure a successful beginning. For instance, the goal might be to talk with four or five different parents each week.

After a student completed a fine drawing of our school, I had postcards printed with the design. I supplied teachers with 10 stamped postcards and asked them to send cards to parents of children who were doing a good job. Community reaction was very positive. Teachers immediately wanted more cards. After a few positive encounters, benefits become apparent. Whatever the technique, parent involvement begins with contact and communication. As Henderson (1988) clearly concluded, "Parent involvement is neither a quick fix nor a luxury; it is absolutely fundamental to a healthy system of public education" (p. 153).

School Operations Must Be
Localized to Meet Community Needs

Schools responsive to the needs of their community are less likely to experience violent behavior. For schools to truly change their 1800s format, every established paradigm must be examined. What hours should school be open to better serve students? What curricular approaches will better serve the needs of students in our community? Changing the school calendar can reduce the number of students in attendance in overcrowded settings at any given week.

Schools without excessive enrollments are moving to modified calendars to better serve their communities. Within many homes, students do not receive any kind of cognitive stimulation during summer vacation. There are no books to read, no trips to the library or museum, and often not even any conversation. Many students subsist on a summer diet of television. When the lack of stimulation is combined with students who are at risk for success in school, we have groups of students returning to school in the fall further behind than when they left in the spring. Single-track modified calendars allow students to attend school the same number of days, with shorter breaks in between. For instance, they might attend for 9 weeks and have 3 weeks off, in the popular 45/15 plan.

During the 3-week intercession, many districts are providing optional programs for children, at minimal or no charge. Some districts are providing for intervention services during intercession so that children who most need extra time and attention are able to receive it. Tangelo Park Elementary School in Orlando, Florida, offers community programs during intercessions. Field trips, swim programs with youth clubs, agreements with museums for art experiences, and other activities are available year round. A high school in Virginia offers accelerated and college courses within the school setting during intercession. Many students are able to graduate from high school with a semester's worth of college credit. That head start may be the factor that encourages a student to pursue a college degree.

Many schools offer before- and after-school programs to serve daycare needs within the community. High schools must explore school classes beginning at 7:00 through 10:00 p.m., if that would best meet the needs of students. Many high school students have to work in the evening or in the morning and would be more likely to stay in school if they had an option on when they could attend. Other high school students are parents and have child care difficulties that contribute to poor attendance. They eventually drop out of school rather than fail.

Teachers might work 10-hour days. A more realistic planning model would have teachers with classes on three 10-hour days, with their fourth day for planning or making home visits. Alternative time options may meet more needs of more students than the traditional model.

What if the school were open 6 days a week? What kind of opportunities for learners, apprenticeships, teachers, businesses, and climate might this present? Students might have options in attending 3 days out of a 6-day week, with an apprenticeship on the fourth day.

Other needs of the community are being met with full-service schools, or schools offering integrated services. Federal, state, and local agencies providing services to families and children could be housed in schools for more effective articulation of solutions to problems. Family counseling services could be made available. Immunization would be available where children are already located. With the school as the center of so many communities, the blend seems like a natural.

Final Thoughts

Glasser (1990) warns that though our best secondary schools may not have an explosive atmosphere, an undercurrent exists full of sullen antagonism. He calls for elimination of the boss-management mentality, because it does not consider the needs of students. "We need to accept the fact that the majority of boss-managed students see little chance of satisfying their needs by working hard in school, and we cannot boss them into doing more" (p. 433).

The least successful schools handle discipline in the most physical ways. Brute strength and force determine who is in charge, rather than teaching and modeling problem solving in a cooperative, collegial way. In the best interest of children and in the best interest of promoting a safe and orderly school environment, school leadership has to be dynamic in its mixture and strength.

Involving Students in
Establishing a Safe School

On at least one morning in every student's life, there was an attempt to find an excuse for not going to school. For some, there might be fear about an element in the school setting; others might be fearful about having to take a test or facing the consequences for some action from the previous day. Commonly, reaction from classmates is a source of fear. Fortunately, most students don't fear anything greater than embarrassment over something as temporary as a haircut that might generate taunts or laughter. At the other extreme are students who live with continual harassment or are attending school in an environment so full of tension and aggression that they continually wonder when they will be the next victim. A survey conducted by the National School Safety Center found that 800,000 students stay home from school one day a month because of fear (Landen, 1992).

Most children's greatest fear is aggression from other children, with one third of actual assaults on children occurring at school

(Cohen & Wilson-Brewer, 1991). Daily worry about getting to school, moving to and from classes, going to the restroom, having lunch, and returning home safely becomes too much of a strain to bear. Fear leads to an inability to concentrate; and when lack of attention is coupled with poor attendance, grades and achievement suffer. Eventually the strain must end. When living with daily fear becomes too much to handle, students decide to end the tension in one way or another. Alternatives available include some of the following options:

- The tension is ended by dropping out of school.
- Due to easy access to a weapon, lack of other apparent possibilities, and/or modeling problem-solving behavior from one's environment, violent retaliation is selected.
- Joining a gang is another route to gain a feeling of security and acceptance in a group.
- Suicide sometimes appears to be the only answer. The suicide rate for 15- to 19-year-olds has tripled in the past 30 years, with 6% of teens attempting suicide (O'Neil, 1991). A study in rural Tennessee, probably not atypical of other schools, found that 31% of students in one high school had considered suicide.

These drastic and detrimental measures finally become more attractive than living with daily tension and fear.

Strategies for Principals to Assist Students to Feel Safe at School

1. Remove the 2% to 5%.
2. Assure students of their rights and responsibilities.
3. Involve students through formal and informal strategies.
4. Implement curriculum to help students solve problems, develop social skills, and resolve conflict.
5. Extend counseling services to all students, and free counselors to counsel.
6. Involve students in developing plans to reduce violence.

7. Extend extracurricular opportunities.

8. Develop the concept of community service as part of each student's ethos.

Remove the 2% to 5%

A very small percentage of the student population creates fear, harasses, intimidates, extorts, and assaults other students. Aggressive children lack the ability to solve problems or to see alternative solutions absent of violence. They lack the ability to accept responsibility and they blame others for their behavior. They ignore or deny the feelings of their victims.

Aggression is a learned behavior that can be changed. Aggressive students need settings that create different possibilities for their behavior. Even very young students can exhibit deviant, bullying behavior and will hurt and intimidate other children. Behavior that is calculated indicates that help is needed. Purposefully torturing or harming small animals is also a warning that professional counseling is immediately required (Sinclair & Alexson, 1992).

A small percentage of students will need additional services to include:

- direction for getting along with others
- guidance toward vocational possibilities
- mentoring programs
- and specific counseling strategies to sort through the combinations of their early environment that created such anger and hostility toward others

Several programs provide options for student difficulties. Schools in Milwaukee established alternative programs for students with repeated incidents toward others. In New York City the Alternative to Incarceration Program establishes opportunities for community service for students convicted of school crimes (Stover, 1988).

Academic achievement and success must be central to any offerings within alternative structures. Classroom experiences and experiences from any mentoring, apprentice, or work program should be reciprocally developed for increased enhancement of both settings. Basic tenets of successful alternative programs include:

- Students with the potential to dropout or dropouts in reentry programs must be taught how to read.
- The learning environment should not feel like the classroom settings in which the students have already failed.
- The teachers in the alternative setting must care (Hahn, 1987). They must possess a large repertoire of teaching approaches compatible to the challenges and learning needs of students who have been unsuccessful in traditional programs.
- Their goals should be more comprehensive and probably more defined and widely understood by students and staff than in the regular high school program.
- Alternative programs are usually smaller. Smaller size reduces the depersonalizing, restrictive, and uniformity dimensions found in larger institutions that often are necessarily bureaucratic.

Although alternative programs are ideally designed to intervene before a student gets into trouble, some are established in conjunction with a school suspension program. Suspension in which students are banished from the school because of unacceptable behavior has not been found to produce any benefit (Comerford & Jacobson, 1987). Not only does the suspension option not benefit students, but studies also consistently demonstrate that suspension is a harmful process. Suspended students commonly are sent back to a home with no supervision, resulting in a high probability that their time will be used in detrimental ways. Out-of-school suspension is negative for a variety of reasons:

- Most suspended students are left unsupervised, resulting in increased opportunities to become involved in criminal behavior. In Jacksonville, Florida, one study found that 64% of juvenile crime was committed by suspended students (Fish, 1993).
- Unsupervised time also contributes to teen pregnancy rates.
- Suspension leads to academic failure, compounding the downward spiral.

As harmful as suspension is for students, there are small numbers of students whose behavior is extreme enough that they will harm others. Their extreme behavior usually means that the justice system is involved by their early teen years. School is an inappropriate place for them. Occasionally, courts attempt to use the school as a holding cell until prison space is available for juvenile offenders.

Stories among principals commonly relate their delay tactics in admitting convicted felons to school, knowing that if they can stall long enough, another crime will be committed. With any luck, the felon may be back in a local jail, awaiting another trial.

> Jerome, a 13-year-old, was brought to school by his parole officer on a Friday in early October. The student had not been in school that academic year. His record to date included a stolen car conviction, robbing a convenience store and beating the clerk, and assorted other charges of battery and small thefts. Because prison space was not available, the parole officer needed a place to keep him busy for at least a month. Our middle school was selected. We used attendance roadblocks to stall admitting Jerome. Immunization records were not in his file, so the parole officer left with plans to return on Monday with the proper records. On Saturday the student stabbed his stepmother as she cooked his breakfast. He stole his father's truck, wrecking it in a chase with the police. On Monday Jerome was back in jail.

> Bryan, angry over a breakup with his girlfriend, left his class, went to his truck, and pulled his sawed-off shotgun out from under the seat. During class time, it was simple for him to move from the parking lot, back through the school corridors, and into his girlfriend's classroom. Bryan entered, held the gun on the shocked students, and demanded that his girlfriend leave with him. As he turned to leave with her, the teacher tackled him. The gun was secured, and Bryan was arrested and taken away. He was questioned, charged, and released. During the last class period of the day, Bryan returned to the school with a knife in his hand. This time he was caught on the grounds before he reached the building.

The security of the majority of students cannot be jeopardized by having court systems return criminals to schools. Our school population should not be subjected to this kind of endangerment.

Assure Students of
Their Rights and Responsibilities

Conduct codes must be established and uniformly distributed to assure student awareness, address legal ramifications, and demonstrate the effort to maintain a safe environment. Review of the code should be held in each classroom at the beginning of the year. Videotape reviews should be part of the orientation of each new student. Codes should be sent home to each parent or guardian, with sign-off forms completed to verify that the code was received. Good conduct codes clearly outline expected behavior and consequences for failing to behave properly. Students should participate in code and amendment development.

Within the classroom, students' active involvement in establishing behavioral expectations and rules will strengthen commitment to a positive environment. Classroom committees, constitutions, and even courts become a deterrent to unacceptable behavior. Improved school outcomes are evidenced when classroom teachers have employed group planning. In an atmostphere where rewards for improved behavior and academic success are emphasized, as opposed to classrooms where attention is derived from punishment for negative behavior, improved behavior occurs (Rich, 1992).

Involve Students Through
Formal and Informal Strategies

Class officers, student councils, and other traditional processes allow students to have some voice in school governance. Participation in school decision making and efforts to prevent violence must go well beyond structures for the few. Crime watches can be organized, similar to Neighborhood Watch. Students present forums, produce videotapes, and present other performances to illustrate alternatives to violence.

Community service activities develop new understandings for students about their role in a world with peaceful coexistence. Community service is a strong model of responsibility for members of the neighborhood. Students might elect to sponsor projects to improve the environment with river cleanup, or help the homeless, or read to the elderly, or some other worthwhile goal either within or beyond their immediate community. For difficulties within the school, student courts are used in many schools to consider student problems (Modglin, 1989). Democratic processes developed by students can have an effect on responses to other problem solving. These school judicial experiences can have a long-term effect on influencing career choices. Middle school field trips to courts and prisons also leave impressions beyond mere civics lessons.

Participation and connection to governance in some schools may include establishing dialogue with groups traditionally regarded as the enemy. In some urban settings, principals have organized peace conferences with leaders from local gangs. A beginning goal is to declare the school a neutral zone. Ideally, the hope would be for initial dialogue to influence reduction of violence throughout the community.

Reviewing our failures can often help us create more successes in the future. Valuable information to help all children can be learned by studying dropouts. Primarily, students drop out of school because they have no opportunity to feel successful or to feel that they are part of the school community. Some children have no advocate and no one to teach them problem-solving skills in any segment of their lives. By changing many of the elements that cause students to drop out of school, principals create a setting that enhances the educational experience of every student.

Purposeful processes must be in place to continually determine the morale and climate of the student body. During the second week of school at Evans High School in Orlando, the principal asked that teachers send students from their second period class to see him. The only criteria for selection for the first session was that the student should be someone whose name the teacher did not yet know. This stipulation eliminated the popular students, the athletes, and the problem students. It did reach the quiet, new, and underrepresented segments.

Every 2 weeks the principal used this forum as a formal means to take the pulse of student perceptions, feelings, concerns. Students could ask any questions they wanted, and different students attended each week. After the first few sessions, students started supplying their class representatives with questions to take along. Students reported the main points from each forum back to classmates.

A caring, committed teacher may be the greatest determiner of whether students become involved in school and in learning. The best teachers are able to demonstrate caring while simultaneously being task oriented. This powerful combination models the importance of learning while considering the student as essential to the process.

Implement Curriculum to Help Students
Solve Problems, Develop Social Skills, and Resolve Conflict

The hidden curriculum is the strongest curriculum for counteracting aggression and violence. The undocumented reactions and actions of the adults in the school environment are influential. Through their daily example, teachers and staff demonstrate acceptance of diversity, respect for each student, strategies to handle frustration and pressure, improvement orientation, and general attitude toward life.

In some communities formal curricular programs and strategies are useful to complement solid values and positive climate existing in the school. Formal packages are available from several agencies and consultants. They commonly contain a sequenced set of lessons to create an awareness about violence within one's environment. Lessons to resolve, prevent, and avoid violence are usually included. Role playing, simulations, videos, and other materials are widely available. Teaching students problem solving, social skills, and conflict resolution are central to most programs and are skill areas with broad application to many areas. Typical elements of these three skill areas follow.

Problem Solving. Many people know only to fight or flee when they encounter something unfamiliar or new. Random attempts or giving up entirely are the experiences many of our students have had at solving problems. Problem-solving skills are essential for every student, whether dealing with approaches to academic challenges or problems encountered in daily life. Many problem-solving strategies are found in textbooks. Each requires a commitment on the part of the teacher to spend time teaching and practicing the procedure, especially when the concept is initially encountered. Careful work at the beginning will assure fuller and more successful use of the strategy. Ecksel (1992, p. 27) suggests the following 11-step approach:

1. Stop and think.
2. Identify the problem.
3. Select a goal.
4. Decide on a goal.
5. Think of solutions (brainstorming).
6. Consider the consequences.
7. Choose the best solution.
8. Evaluate all alternatives.
9. Try the plan.
10. Evaluate the outcome.
11. If the first fails, try another plan.

Practice within the classroom can allow any problem-solving approach to be incorporated into the students' repertoire. The daily newspaper provides a variety of social studies and science examples for applications of the process. Such exercises are ideal for cooperative learning approaches that build students' appreciation of one another's skills and talents. Brainstorming for solutions, or 26 heads are better than one, demonstrates strength gathered in alliances.

Social Skills. A lack of social skills is often a reason for behavior leading to aggression. Many students have no way of knowing how to deal with their peers. They have no experience with responding to humor or teasing. They don't attempt to understand the actions of another person. Something like accidentally bumping into someone in the school hallway can result in retaliation. Disagreements at home were settled with hitting, and the same technique is utilized at school. Calmly discussing an issue is unfamiliar; perhaps no one has ever discussed the need to control anger or emotions.

Positive Adolescent Choices Training (PACT) in Dayton, Ohio, assists students in learning social skills (Hammond, 1990). Social skills within the training include:

1. Giving positive feedback. Students learn how and when to thank or compliment other people.
2. Giving negative feedback. Students find appropriate ways to disagree and criticize. They learn ways to express disappointment.
3. Accepting negative feedback. They practice listening and attempting to understand criticism.
4. Resisting peer pressure. Students develop a strategy for not following the behavior of a group.
5. Problem solving. They learn problem-solving approaches.
6. Negotiation. Students practice resolving conflicts, developing solutions, and learning to compromise.

Purposeful lessons on such basic behavior are essential for many of our students to learn to get along without violence.

Conflict Resolution. Conflicts often result from competition, misunderstanding of verbal and nonverbal signals, prejudice, a lack of respect for others, and an inability to properly vent hurt, abuse, or anger. Students needing recognition and a feeling of power in their lives will resort to conflict to get it. School districts throughout the country have initiated programs to counter these sources of conflict. For example, The Boston Conflict Resolution Program works with teachers and students. Trained teachers are supported within the classroom with multiethnic teams to implement the program (U.S. Department of Health and Human Services, 1993).

Schools in Portland, Oregon, trained students as conflict managers in a 15-hour program composed of problem-solving and communication skills. They were available to offer assistance to students who encounter conflict. Though some districts train students as peer mediators, other experts do not feel that students should be involved in defusing potentially violent encounters (Ordovensky, 1993).

Extend Counseling Services to All Students, and Free Counselors to Counsel

Patterns of deviant behavior begin at very early ages and are visible during the child's years in elementary school. When no counseling services are available until middle school, behavior will have escalated, and the adolescent will have construced firm walls to prevent change from occurring (Dodge, 1992). Various patterns of counseling approaches must be tailored to the needs of the school setting. Possibilities for group counseling topics include dealing with grief, coping strategies for children of alcoholics, programs for overweight students, eating disorder programs, and coping with parents who are divorcing. Classroom counseling can assist the teacher with hostility problems and students struggling to learn how to make friends.

Videos also can provide a strong assist to any counseling program. To counteract media messages in which people magically recover after being shot, videotapes using gunshot victims are shown in some school systems to emphasize the pain and cost of violence.

Involve Students in Plans to Reduce Violence

McCoy Elementary School in Orlando, Florida, adopted the theme, "Kindness Is Spoken Here." Instituting that motto helped make important things happen. Because many children do not understand the dimensions of kindness, awareness was a necessary foundation. Our guidance counselor gathered students to perform skits on the morning video. Two or three children demonstrated kind acts. Students were invited to submit examples of kindness for skits they produced or others acted. Examples evolved into a program through which students could nominate other students for the "I Made a Difference" award. Nominated students were presented with a ribbon on the morning video show. Their parents were called and informed of their child's good actions. Pictures of nominated students were placed on a monthly roster by the school's front door. Our four-word theme had wide-ranging effects on attitudes in our school and community.

From such elementary school beginnings, campaigns at middle and high school levels are possible. Joint themes through all feeder schools might establish a communications link, as well as awareness and participation for students. Districtwide themes selected from student-generated ideas are a starting point.

Organized campaigns, club projects, and spontaneous class assignments afford students a chance to participate in reducing violence within their school environment. In addition to such proactive approaches, spontaneity is sometimes necessary. After a man attempted to lure two students into a car, we quickly pulled together all of our students who walked home. We requested that they organize themselves into teams and devise plans on how they would walk to and from school in groups. Additionally, they worked together to select the most populated and open routes. Some schools have organized "safe spots" within each block. Certain houses, carefully screened by the school, receive signs to post in their windows. Children in trouble or hurt know that they are safe to approach such designated houses. Programs organizing safe strategies for going to and from school are important considerations for students of any age.

Extend Extracurricular Opportunities

The impact of extracurricular opportunities on students was never more clearly conveyed than on one hot August afternoon as we watched football practice. We were amazed to see one particular player on the field that day. His father had died the night before. Since being released from prison the previous week, his father had been hiding in an abandoned house. The drug dealers he had shortchanged found him, shot him, and torched the building. When the coach came over, we asked about why Andy was at practice. The coach had had the same question. Andy replied that football was his only ticket away from what had happened to his father. It was his one chance at a scholarship and college. He did not feel he could afford to miss a practice.

Extracurricular activities embody great potential for many students. Being a member of the band is often the only reason some students stay in school, behave properly, and maintain a C average. The same can be said for all other extracurricular activities. A sport or activity provides:

- a connection for some students to relate to other students
- a chance to feel that they are part of the larger scheme of schooling
- a way to be successful
- a connection to associate with an adult with enthusiasm around something meaningful
- an occasion to practice, develop, and refine social skills
- an opportunity to explore a new interest, reach for a hidden talent, find a hobby
- a shot at a scholarship, career possibility, or recognition
- a chance to develop increasing levels of maturity and responsibility

Two major considerations are involved with extracurricular activities: funding and participation. For instance, band and football programs are very expensive extracurricular activities when calculated on a per student basis. Other activities, such as a baseball card club, chess club, ham radio club, future problem-solving team, dance group, and a hundred other options can involve many of the less involved students within a school and require much less funding for support.

Another big participation issue surrounds transportation. Students who are bused to school are often in situations where they cannot participate in extracurricular activities. A Communities in Schools group in one town secured grant funding to provide city bus transportation home one hour after the middle school day for students needing it. Students who do not have parents who can transport them from after-school activities are often the ones who need that type of connection, success, and exploration the most. School leadership must make every effort to find solutions to create access for all students.

Develop the Concept of Community Service
as Part of Each Student's Ethos

Concerted effort has to be made to connect a large percentage of our student population to their community. Frequent school changes are routine for children of the disenfranchised; and adjusting to a new school each year constitutes reality for many students. Broward County,

Florida, found a transient rate in its high schools that averaged seven moves per student (Rossilini, 1988). For legal, cultural, or economic reasons, many children have never witnessed examples of community participation, club membership, or volunteerism. Again, the school may furnish the only opportunity to build such connections.

Community service plans in some areas are developed to provide an extracurricular experience. Other plans involve the student in an internship experience, contributing to a community agency. Graduation requirements in an increasing number of states, including Maryland and Georgia, require completing certain numbers of hours of community service.

Community service creates a variety of positive connections for students. In parks, nursing homes, or other settings, they have the opportunity to bond with adults who exhibit models of success, work ethic, and problem solving. They can often learn specific job skills and gain a sense of the behavior expected in work settings. Community service is a chance for many students to experience success and positive interactions.

Community service is an occasion to practice caring about other people. Some schools have partnerships with homes for the elderly or child care centers. Schools close to parks take responsibility for painting projects or shelter construction. "Clean Streams" campaigns in other areas have channeled student energy into removing debris from riverbanks. Serving food in shelters, reading stories to homeless children, or bagging sand against a flood allow the humane and decent parts of each person to dominate. The plight of the weaker elements of our communities, and the paths that created their dilemmas, serve as strong lessons for students.

Final Thoughts

When schools involve students in developing the rules and procedures under which they will function, an opportunity is fostered for them to become more responsible. A school setting rich in possibilities and experiences with a caring climate creates a setting for student growth.

5

Involving the Community and Parents

Community Involvement

The relationship between school violence and violence within the community maintains a chicken-and-egg cyclical quality. One affects the other, and spending time looking for a place to assign blame at any given moment is purely academic. To reduce the potential of violence within the school and the community, the principal's time and energy are more proactively and effectively expended by increasing communication and understanding between the school and the community.

The importance of enhancing relationships between schools and their communities has recently gained national attention. Studies of schools of excellence emphasize good schools with long traditions of working cooperatively within their community. A safe school should be viewed as a community campaign. The school influences activities throughout the community and should not be regarded as being isolated. Increasingly schools are being seen as an integral part of a

58 CREATING SAFE SCHOOLS

larger community, and the school principal becomes the connecting influence in this relationship.

The national recognition of the importance of community and school collaboratives was emphasized when the United States Department of Education and the United States Department of Health and Human Services published *Together We Can* (Melaville & Blank, 1993). This book explores the relationships of schools and human service agencies working together for the benefit of children and families. The model presented maintains that children and families must be the primary consideration and focus for learning to happen in communities. Closest to supporting the family are members of the extended family, friends, and neighbors. The school is identified in relationship to churches, hospitals, and other agencies as helping institutions. Crisis agencies and treatment services are found at the next level of support. Clearly, expectations for the role of the school have changed. With the principal in the role of community leader, schools are now viewed as integral and pivotal connections in:

- bringing about change in communities
- connecting agencies within the community
- helping not only children but also their families

Greater awareness of the importance of school and family/community collaboration has spread for several reasons:

- Today's problems with students have escalated in number and intensity. It has become essential that many sources work together to find solutions to the problems.
- There is now a positive view toward collaboration as an acceptable and preferred way to solve problems. Former sentiment viewed it as a sign of weakness and incompetence when schools received help from other directions. The end of "Lone Ranger" leadership mentality has assisted in this change.
- Revenues and resources continue to become increasingly scarce. Taxpayers are intensifying their pressure for more responsive service and responsible government spending.

- Special interest groups influence school policy and actions as well as governmental behavior.
- Various foundations have created a financial impetus to work together. Funding is often based on demonstrated collaboration with various constituencies.
- There are idenfitiable past successes when families responded and improvement occurred after agencies and schools "accidentally" coordinated their efforts.
- When students' needs are being met, frustration exhibited in angry and violent behavior is reduced. It is more likely that needs will be met when school programs are collaboratively developed.

New Roles for the Principal

The principal is instrumental in establishing an environment of receptivity within the school for changes that are occurring. Faculty and staff need to be assisted in changing from the traditional isolated structure that is still found within many schools. The vision building talents of the principal become critical at this point, as the staff struggles to see what the new picture of the school can be. The bumpy spots along the way can be overcome when effort is made to create occasions to reflect, commit to structure, establish ownership, and celebrate progress.

Beyond the circle of their own faculty, principals become facilitators who integrate schools and communities. They are sought out to provide direction and establish focus, relying on skills in trust building, strategic planning, team building, and organizing. Their expertise will be tested in the search for linkages between goals and resources.

In the pages ahead, examples and other specifics regarding new roles for schools and the new challenges for contemporary principals will be explored. These directions include new roles for the school, partnerships with parents, and partnerships with other members of the community.

New Roles for the School

The School as Setting of Integrated Services

During the night, fire destroyed a home in our school community. By noon the next day, food, clothing, and money had been delivered to our school office to assist the family in need. The school was viewed as a trusted and helping entity. Schools are often perceived as the natural nucleus of many communities. When the wagons are circled, the school is commonly in the center.

Schools then are logically evolving as the center for networking governmental services for families. If children need immunization to enter school, offering health services at the school makes sense. Schools are often geographically convenient and accessible. Many have space available for adding offices. They sit on land already owned by taxpayers, and, usually, are recognized as being interested in collaborating with families for the welfare of children.

Principals and teachers have long known that troubled children are merely the symptom of a deeper problem; dysfunctional families create at-risk students. Improved education for troubled children requires work with the entire family. The most convenient and direct way to reach families with counseling and intervention services is to offer them within the school.

Parenting support is the most natural assistance that schools contribute to the larger family unit. This type of assistance ranges from support and information classes for parents of students to day care for the children of students. Here are but two among many successful examples:

> In an effort to prevent drug use in high-risk children, Broward County Schools conducts parenting classes. Primary objectives of the program include development of more effective communication skills and increased sensitivity toward children's needs. Efforts are made to expand the understanding of the parents about the supportive role they can play, rather than isolating their role to that of disciplinarian. Special support is given to the multiple difficulties of single parents. Family therapy is also available (Rossilini, 1988).

NASSP Bulletin has highlighted parent outreach efforts that have proven successful. The Staten Island Project is one such endeavor. Parent groups were organized to allow them to examine their interactions with their children. Sessions also concentrated on communication, positive family relationships, and handling stress. They further explored decision-making alternatives among the parent and child, with special emphasis on understanding adolescent development. Another major program objective was to help participants acquire a group identity, with efforts at fostering mutual support. More positive relationships with the school became a bonus of this program (Jackson & Cooper, 1992).

Many high schools offer day care for the children of their students. Allied services are also available. Services for teen fathers and mothers include discipline strategies, lessons on reading to their children, nutrition information, and medical assistance. One program found it necessary to teach students nursery rhymes, lullabies, and peek-a-boo, because they had never experienced this part of childhood and could not pass it along to their children.

Reviewing successful programs that provide services to families reveals that there is no standard formula. Good programs recognize the transitional nature of the needs of the community and the dynamic nature of community resources. New roles between agencies and for schools will evolve and probably merge in intricate forms during the next few years. Ideally, individual models will continue to form to meet the needs of various communities.

Kadel and Follman (1993) produced a list of agencies and their possible contributions (see Box 5.1). This list might be useful to principals when formulating programs to integrate community services. It is also useful to establish initial connections.

The School in Partnership With Parents and Other Community Members

One million people volunteered their services to public schools during the 1987-1988 school year. About 60% of public schools in the

BOX 5.1

List of Agencies and Their Possible Contributions

Agency	Possible Contributions
Social service providers	Counseling, conflict resolution, parent education
Early childhood specialists	Identifying child abuse, locating learning problems, social skills
Mental health counseling	Counseling for chemical abuse and other dysfunctional behaviors
Medical practitioners	Expertise on health issues, first aid, and CPR training
Court and probation officers	Legal alternatives and advice, programs for students
Parks and recreation staff	Alternatives to violence, resources for students
State government officials	Expertise on alternative and supplementary resources, technical assistance, availability of resources

United States capitalize on this valuable resource (Michael, 1990). This league of one million-plus volunteers contributes precious time, expertise, resources, experience, caring, and talent to collaborate in the shared responsibility of helping children succeed in school. Their presence in schools presents students with models of additional adults in their world, helping students learn that education is valued by many people.

Benefits in this relationship are reciprocal. The self-esteem of volunteers is enhanced when they see students' learning improve because of their efforts. Many volunteer programs involve the elderly within the community, or are developed around specific partnerships with nursing homes. The elderly can assist young children beginning to read by working with sight word drill or reading stories. One program pairs teens with musically talented residents of a nursing home for assistance with music lessons.

Retired people who held jobs as engineers, operated businesses, or served in the military have an arsenal of powerful skills and talents to offer. Beginning the first week of school each year, one elderly man in our community works with each kindergartner until every child constructs his or her very own birdhouse. This ritual takes the entire school year. For many of our students, this is the closest they come to interacting with a grandparent. A volunteer program in one high school uses retired people to discuss job skills with seniors and put them through mock interviews. High school vocational classes have natural links with retired persons who have a variety of skills.

Studies of at-risk students have found that 10% to 20% break out of the poverty cycle and become successful, productive adults. The most significant factor for the students breaking the cycle was their relationship with one person who believed in them. Most commonly this person was an educator. It would seem that effective mentoring programs might raise the percentages of at-risk children who become successful adults. Mentoring programs with one-to-one relationships between a student and an adult are especially beneficial and hold a powerful potential.

By conveying a belief that the student can succeed, a mentor can establish the vital link to change a student's negative direction. A ninth grader with a terrible attendance record never missed school on Wednesday, because that was her time to talk with her mentor. A 15-year-old boy decided to run away from home because his relationship with his stepfather was full of conflict. Before he left town, he stopped to tell his mentor goodbye and was coaxed into staying and trying again.

Establishing cultural programs and celebrations not only enriches the curriculum but also extends global understandings for students. Involving community members from diverse cultures in school activities humanizes the differences in our society. After firsthand contact with immigrants from other regions, students soon learn that stereotypes are not viable. These approaches reduce tension among diverse groups within the school. The hope is that such experiences will be translated into understanding of other differences in people. Following a cross-cultural event, one high school student was asked what he thought of the Iranian he had just met. He replied, "He was just a regular person."

Another benefit of increased numbers of volunteers equates to increased numbers of citizens supporting school funding. Volunteers (a.k.a. taxpayers) see the dedication and professional work that occur in schools. Their accounts of school successes ripple through the community.

Parent Partnerships

Benefits are even greater for students when the volunteers are their parents. Henderson (1987) reviewed more than 50 studies that examined the effects of parent involvement in schools. She found overwhelming support for parent involvement in almost any form relating to increased student achievement. In studies of volunteer programs in which parent involvement was the only difference, parent involvement produced greater gains. When parents' attitudes toward school improve, children's views of school are enhanced. Regardless of cultural and economic background, children whose parents become involved with the school make greater achievement gains. More powerfully, the effects last for years as students move through school. Some of the major effects include "higher grades and test scores, better long-term academic achievement, positive attitudes and behavior, more successful programs, and more effective schools" (Henderson, 1988, p. 149).

Ripple benefits into the community often occur. An unemployed father of a track athlete hung around every afternoon to watch practice. The coach asked him to assist on some measuring and recording tasks. The assistance grew until he became a vital part of the track coaching staff. After he was told about available resources to help him complete his high school diploma, he successfully completed the GED and was able to get a job. Benefits from parent involvement are certainly reciprocal.

Parent Involvement
Connected to Reducing Violence

Parents can also make a significant impact in reducing school crime. Parents at a high school in La Puente, California, began patrolling the campus and cafeteria in 1981. The crime rate was cut by one half (Foley, 1990). The mere presence of adult figures in most settings can translate into improved student behavior. An important model is presented to students when they see parents interested enough in education to volunteer their time.

The performance of both teachers and children improves in a setting enhanced by support, attention, and assistance. When these positive factors are present in the school atmosphere, conditions supporting violence, aggression, and harm subside.

Connections between reducing violence within schools and school volunteer programs, especially parent involvement programs, seem clear. Further extensive communication needs to occur between the principal and citizens in homes or businesses surrounding the school. The school needs to support concerns of those citizens regarding students' behavior. Conversely, support of campus neighbors should be enlisted. The school's neighbors can be asked to report unusual behavior, cars with drivers watching the schools, or strangers entering school property. Activity viewed from such vantage points as neighboring buildings can be the first alert to the school that people are on the roof, a student is hiding behind a trash bin, or that two people are in a car in the parking lot.

Memphis City Schools put together a task force of community, school, and business representatives to address increased violence within their schools. Conclusions of the task force contained repeated recommendations for community involvement. Their findings, summarized in *Report of the School Violence Task Force* (1993) called for the involvement of parents in a variety of ways, including:

- increasing school volunteerism
- increasing male role models in schools by involving parents and community members
- involving parents in program development

- developing safety patrols of parents, grandparents, and other citizens
- enlisting community members for bathroom and hall patrols

Two Factors to Consider

1. All parents are interested in their children's school success and happiness. Differences do exist in parental ability to demonstrate their interest. Parents of achieving, middle-class, elementary school children are easy to involve in school activities. They arrive for parent conferences, join PTA, send cookies, volunteer for school council memberships, observe teaching, request input in their students' classroom placement, contribute to discussion and decision making about curriculum, and participate in fund-raising and special events.

School involvement drastically diminishes for a variety of other parents and guardians. When the parents do not speak English, belong to a minority not represented among adults at the school, do not have transportation, are in legal trouble, are illiterate, have a student who does not want them at school, or are constrained by a variety of other conditions, they are less likely to participate in activities surrounding their child's school.

To change this pattern, principals must put several strategies in place.

- A nonintimidating essence must surround each school's volunteer program.
- Parents must be able to contribute in a variety of ways. Like students, parents need to experience success. When carefully planned, this is entirely possible for parents who are illiterate or do not speak English.
- Careful training must take place which maintains the dignity of each volunteer (Zajdel, 1993).
- A member of the school staff with excellent interaction skills should be responsible for organizing, training, providing feedback, and follow through for the entire program. Commitment of this allocation and planning time is imperative.

- Opportunities should be available for parents to assist from their homes. Transportation to school is a problem for some parents. Some systems permit volunteers to ride to and from school on school buses; others have arranged for free or low-cost fares on public transportation.

- Planning for a comprehensive volunteer program should involve representatives of the many constituencies within the school.

- All parents must be aware of how they can participate and must be asked, probably more than once. Communication must be two-way. Information can be disseminated within the community at common meeting areas, such as fast-food restaurants, grocery stores, and churches (Jennings, 1992).

- Teachers and other staff members should receive training in effective ways to utilize volunteers to enhance student achievement. Burke (1991) felt that teachers are in the most important "position to erect these bridges to the community" (p. 13).

2. Students from impoverished and/or minority families benefit the most when their parents become involved in school. A clear picture still forms in my head of a volunteer working in the high school library stacks. She always looked like a timid bird ready for flight. To protect her efforts, a few key people knew that she sneaked to school whenever she thought it was safe. Her husband forbade her to leave the house, but sometimes she took the chance and came to shelve books in our library. We were careful not to have her name on our volunteers' board, and her name never went in the thank you column in the monthly newsletter. We silently hoped that the books would give her courage to change her life.

A picture also forms, totally from imagination, of a Hispanic mother I never got to meet. She volunteered to color and cut out game pieces, awards, and math manipulatives. She had no transportation and spoke no English. Children in her apartment building would take the activities to her on the bus. The examples of individuals like these show what a strong effect volunteering and contributing to the school can have on not only their children but also all children in that environment, now and in the future.

Final Thoughts

When the school is viewed as a community center, direct and indirect support increases. Coordination with government agencies can make family services more attainable and more successful. Family involvement in curricular and support programs infuses valuable sets of hands, perspectives, and ideas into our schools.

Foundations and other grant sources throughout the country are actively supporting the costs of establishing school and community initiatives and parent volunteer programs. The primary catalyst for these positive changes resides within the leadership provided by the school. A welcoming and open attitude, as portrayed by the principal, initiates programs that provide valuable resources for students.

How the Central Office
Can Help Prevent School Violence

Preventing school violence requires addressing the two primary
sources of violence. The most common source of school violence
is pervasive aggressive behavior of students against others in the
school setting. Establishing school climates that prohibit violence
involve coordinated, planned, consistent, and supportive efforts on
the part of a variety of stakeholders. The second source, random
aggression from strangers, requires proactive planning to discourage
the selection of the school as a site for violence. If a tragedy occurs,
crisis planning is essential to minimize damage and harm.

Though factors limiting violence are centralized within each school's
structure, each principal deserves a wider base of support. Proactive
efforts to coordinate and plan begin at the district level. Every school
principal should expect that the district will assume certain responsibilities. These responsibilities include both some basic functions and
increasingly specific services. Essential functions extend to several areas.

District Office Functions Preventing Possibilities of Violence and Fostering Positive School Climate

1. Selecting the most competent principal
2. Enabling communities to grow by forming smaller groups of students
3. Fostering site-based decision making
4. Supporting consistent conduct policies

Selecting the Most Competent Principal

After reviewing an extensive body of research, Gersten, Carnine, and Green (1982) summarized that a "key to enduring, sustained effective educational services is the site administrator—especially the principal" (p. 15). The leadership of the principal affects climate more than any other single dimension. Workplace norms are established by the principal. The level of expectation for student achievement and behavior also stems from standards clarified and modeled by the principal. In regard to attainment of a safe and orderly environment, literature from effective schools research concludes that the role of the principal is the vital element to creating a safe school (Purkey & Smith, 1982).

Assuring the selection of the best candidate for each school principalship is the most important function of the district office. In the real world, this requires that a superintendent be courageous and clever enough to keep school board members and other political factions from dictating the selection of principals. Allowing the principalship to be a vehicle for politicians to return favors can lead to mediocrity or worse.

The essential factor for selection is identifying the most competent leader for each school, and being able to build a sense of community within the school is an essential quality. Lists of leadership competencies, sets of interview questions, selection procedures, and other sound personnel methods are widely available.

After locating a group of competent people, finding the right fit between the principal's style and the needs of each school community becomes the next challenge. Some principals have patience with the underdog and will provide compassionate service to lower socio-economic communities. Other principals excel at creating new dimensions in schools. For them, a school ready for change is ideal. Principals who skillfully maintain a warm, supportive climate are needed in schools that have suffered intense upheaval.

An additional challenge to finding the right fit between school and principal involves adding an assistant principal to the mix. The principal is capable of inspiring and developing the leadership potential of assistant principals. The assistant principalship is an excellent training ground for future leaders for the district.

These critical personnel decisions require careful consideration and assessment. Hiring the most effective school leaders involves a complex series of decisions and procedures; and those in charge of hiring should solicit input from both school personnel and the school's community at every step. Insights from the local setting are imperative if the best fit is to be found.

More difficult personnel decisions involve removing ineffective principals from their positions. When a principal is not experiencing success, there are two alternatives to chose from:

1. The person may need to be moved to a second site to see if another setting will provide a successful match. A support program, with mentors and additional training, may be effective in improving the person's leadership and management skills.

2. In severe situations, ethical responsibility requires removing the person from the principalship.

Actions taken with an ineffective principal represent district sentiment regarding equity and standards of expectation in schools. When an ineffective principal is moved to a less advantaged school, it appears that school is less worthy of good leadership. The same message is given if an ineffective principal is disciplined by being moved from high school to middle school to elementary level. The message that one grade configuration is somehow better or more deserving than another conveys a district standard.

High expectations and standards are communicated throughout the school system when administrators are accountable. Effective personnel selection procedures will minimize the possibility of selecting poor leaders. Hiring procedures for administrative positions, as well as all others in the district, should contain provisions to screen applicants with background problems. Routine fingerprinting in some states eliminates up to 3% of applicants after past criminal records are uncovered.

Further, each district must have a policy of identifying, mentoring, and developing potential leaders. Formal "grow our own" programs to foster future principals, especially candidates from underrepresented groups, are mandated in some states. Programs involve internships, shadowing experiences, teachers as leaders sessions, and specific training workshops.

Finding the most competent principal for each school directly affects the probability of success of every student in the school. There must be action taken to preserve a healthy school climate for all members of the school community. A poorly performing principal in one school also adversely affects other schools in the district. For example, a feeder school to your high school is functioning in an out-of-control atmosphere. Your job is more difficult, because new expectations must be established. It takes a longer time and more personnel effort to achieve acceptable student behavior. In addition, stories about the incompetent principal hurt other administrators. Outlandish tales of unprofessional behavior spread through the community and even appear in the media. Incompetence hurts every professional.

A climate tolerating violent, aggressive behavior toward students and staff has little opportunity to flourish when the principal has the ability to foster formation of a collective vision, and has the leadership to move the school community toward achieving that vision.

Enabling Communities to Grow
by Forming Smaller Groups of Students

Following the primary factor of selecting the right school leader, the size of the population of each school becomes the second critical factor within the prerogative of each school district. Size of the school often determines whether a sense of community can be formed. In the midst of disconnected, adversarial neighbors and streets full of strangers, schools will continue to be the one real possibility for many people to achieve a sense of belonging and community. Good decision making by the school district determines how often this is possible. Schools of thousands of students foster impersonal, mechanized learning factories at best, and chaotic time bombs of violence at worst. School size is a powerful determiner of whether community can happen.

Every strategy for reducing the potential of violence is aggravated by large numbers of students. Some of the complications are as follows:

- Clear, accurate communication becomes more difficult.
- Procedures and policies become more convoluted.
- Hallways and the cafeteria are more congested. Shoving leading to fighting and retaliation is more difficult to suppress.
- Layers of bureaucracy grow. Levels are created between leadership and others within the organization.
- Fewer adults are visible. Supervision is more difficult.
- Campuses and equipment become more worn and difficult to maintain.
- Participatory leadership is increasingly challenging.
- The visions of the school can become blurred in the layers of communication.
- Students and staff lose their identity.
- The principal moves farther from the classroom. He or she is perceived as more remote.
- Fewer students are known by name.
- Odds of participating in extracurricular activities are reduced.

Any semblances of community evaporate in huge settings. Size also complicates the factors that keep students in school and create positive student feelings toward school. For students to stay in school, it is important for them to feel that:

- they are part of the institution
- they are involved in some aspect

- their ideas are heard
- their objectives can be met in this school
- they can participate in the workings of the school
- some adult will know who they are and what they dream

Within a classroom, size is also a factor in the students' sense of community and belonging. The number of students within each classroom makes a difference in the probability of aggression. A National Institute of Education (1978) study found that incidents of aggression increased with class size. Aggression also increased as the number of students whom each teacher taught per week grew.

Ideally, new facilities are constructed to manage growth in school districts. If additional facilities are not possible to reduce the number of students and the size of the geographic region impacted by the school, other configurations are possible.

- Models of *schools within a school* (SWAS) are used in many systems. Commonly, students identified as at risk of dropping out of school are placed into a separate area or building. Lower pupil/teacher ratios and intensive, alternative curricular approaches are common strategies. Some SWAS effectively develop increased student identity through mentoring relationships with successful local business people. Other programs require students to do community volunteer service. Particular aspects of SWAS vary, but the objective of dropout prevention is the same.

- *Interdisciplinary teams* of teachers, especially in middle schools, reduce the size of student groups. Schools divide students into groups of from 100 to 120 to work with a limited number of teachers. Edgewater High School in Orlando, Florida, has six teachers paired with 125 students in 2-hour blocks of time for courses, rather than the typical 55-minute periods. Not only do teachers have closer contact with fewer students but the increased time also encourages variation in curricular approaches. Students experiencing large time blocks are more likely to be involved in the learning process.

- To both reduce size and handle geographic or demographic needs, some systems have *separate schools* for a specific grade level or one or two grades. Some large high schools have split the ninth grade onto a separate campus. Middle schools are sometimes separated into a sixth and seventh grade campus and an eighth and ninth grade campus.
- *Multitrack schedules* are a more complex possibility for reducing the number of students within the school at any one time. Schools with multitrack schedules have students divided into segments. For example, if the student population is in five segments, four would be attending at any one time. Students would rotate in and out of the school on a year-round calendar. This has been a viable option in several districts. Districts that have been successful with multitrack schedules have involved parents throughout every phase of the planning and design.

Whatever the variation, the goal is the same: Students will be more likely to stay in school, meet success, establish a sense of belonging, and not exhibit aggressive behavior if the size of the unit to which they belong is reduced.

Fostering Site-Based Decision Making

Even within the same school district, each school is unique. Many policies need to be flexibly established to meet the special needs of the various school communities. Decisions regarding curriculum, staff development priorities, budget allocations, personnel utilization, and other individual needs should be placed closest to the site of implementation.

In many school systems, school committees have developed different yearly calendars and weekly calendars. According to the National Association for Year Round Education, more than 1.5 million students attended schools with modified calendars during the 1992-1993 school year. An urban high school may best serve student needs by being open from 7:00 a.m. until 10:00 p.m. Students can select morning, afternoon, or evening schedules around their work or child care demands.

A school might serve students better if it were open 6 days a week. The student would have an option of which 4 days to attend. Teachers could teach three 10-hour days and use the fourth day for planning and home visits. The old shipbuilding, agrarian calendar and hours of operation no longer fit most communities very effectively. With massive changes in decision making, the district office becomes a service provider. In the model just described, the district office should support grant writing to get funding for travel expenses and materials needed for home visits. A community liaison director in the district office should establish business support and apprentice programs. The focus of the district office is changing. Central office personnel are emerging as facilitators and coordinators of school change (David, 1989). In brief, the district office is facing massive changes.

Supporting Consistent Conduct Policies

Uniform procedures and understanding must be established throughout the district regarding expectations in dealing with school crime. Aggressive behavior, intimidation, extortion, assault, sexual harassment, and other common forms of school crime cannot be tolerated, denied, or ignored. If these acts are allowed, the frequency and magnitude of crime will continue to increase. Consistently enforcing policy is labor-intensive, but it is critical that procedures are followed.

The superintendent and school board should sponsor development of a code of conduct for the entire system, with student rights and responsibilities carefully outlined. The code should be developed by a representative group of principals, teachers, students, parents, and community members. The final policy must contain clearly defined consequences for unacceptable behavior. Policy created with input from each school will assist in consistent enforcement. Annual reviews of the code are important to amend identified ambiguity or changing needs. For instance, mooning and streaking were offenses during the 1970s and 1980s, but technology infractions are recently establishing chapters in conduct policy.

Consistent expectations regarding student attendance are closely tied to the conduct policy. Students not in school are not progressing academically. Attendance incentive programs must be initiated at the district level, with encouragement, financially or otherwise, to each school to make improved attendance a major goal. Some districts with year-round or modified school calendars are examining possibilities of requiring students with more than 10 days of absence to attend additional days during intercessions. Attendance is too critical a factor for student academic success to not focus considerable district effort toward attaining improved rates of attendance.

District Office Services Reducing Possibilities of Violence and Fostering Positive School Climate

1. Professional development
2. Transportation
3. Maintenance services
4. Permanent substitutes
5. Human resource services
6. Crisis response

Professional Development

Comprehensive staff development is essential to increasing staff awareness. Promoting awareness of areas that could minimize the prospect of violence within the school creates confidence and, if violence occurs, promotes a suitable response. For instance, principals and staff members must receive clear training about school policies regarding criminal behavior. Local law enforcement agencies are often eager to clarify legal aspects. This chance for dialogue also can establish important communication between school personnel and police officers.

A systematic and continuous procedure of training is necessary to both adjust to changes in policy and orient recently hired employees. As a new drug becomes common in the area, training is needed to create awareness concerning its nicknames, its appearance, and the behavior of users.

Other training assists employees and indirectly supports reduction in violent activities. Topics for such training will include:

- Motivating at-risk students

    How do we keep students in school?

    Can the classroom be structured in a different way to involve more students?

    What services are available to assist the classroom teacher in finding success for all students?

- Understanding diversity

    How do various cultures view the responsibility of schools and teachers toward their children?

    What kind of class setting assists students with diverse backgrounds and language understandings to be most successful in school?

    What nonverbal behavior are students from various cultures using to communicate with the teacher?

- Cooperative learning and small-group techniques

    When are cooperative learning and small-group work most appropriate?

    How can all students be involved in group activities?

    What assessment techniques can be used to evaluate individual progress of students involved in group projects?

- Developing responsible learners

    What classroom strategies develop more responsible behavior in students?

    How can providing students with choices in assignment and assessment develop responsibility?

- Teacher teams or peer collaboration

    What techniques are available to facilitate teacher collaboration?

- Law and policy awareness
- Techniques to more effectively communicate with and involve parents
- Suicide awareness

  What are the indicators that a student might be considering suicide?

  If a student commits suicide, how can other students be helped to deal with the situation?

- Counseling techniques
- Conflict and confrontation management

  What techniques can defuse aggressive encounters between students? Between adults?

  What nonverbal behavior helps defuse a tense situation?

- Chemical dependency

  What types of behavior indicate a student is suffering from chemical dependency?

  What types of behavior indicate a student is living in a home that is dysfunctional due to chemical dependency?

- Crisis management

  What is the role of each staff member during an emergency?

  What are the plans for the school and students under various emergency situations?

- Alternative approaches to classroom management
- First aid, CPR, emergency treatment
- Crime prevention

  What personal behavior should I exhibit so as not to become a crime victim?

Each district should have a professional development committee widely representing the district staff. Members will serve as the communication vehicle for more comprehensive involvement. With greater involvement, perceived needs of staff members and the needs of the district are more likely to be met.

Transportation

Realistic transportation routes reduce possibilities for violent behavior. Every principal knows that sensible schedules contribute to smoother beginnings and endings for the school day. Excessively long routes, extended periods between arrival and class beginning times, or after school before bus pickups, create blocks of unstructured time that can lead to negative behavior. The school day has a chance for a calmer tone when the transportation director carefully devises the schedule and trains bus drivers in student management as well as driving technique. Random video monitoring installed in buses in some districts has improved student behavior. Safer conditions are created when drivers spend less time dealing with discipline and experience greater opportunity to concentrate on their driving.

Analysis of bus referrals quickly illustrates patterns of where problems exist. Seventy-three percent of the bus behavior problems leading to referrals at our school were from one of the 14 buses serving us. Further investigation identified no correlation with the students being referred and any other problems with behavior in or out of the classroom. When the source of the problem became clear, the transportation director found the driver a more compatible route.

Maintenance Services

If responsibility for maintenance of facilities rests at the district level, every effort must be made to provide equitable and efficient service. Clean, orderly facilities and campus areas contribute to pride within the school and community. The time of school personnel can be better used in classrooms or throughout the campus than with working through layers of bureaucratic forms required to get simple repairs, lawn care, or painting completed.

A few districts are examining the cost-effectiveness of supporting responsibility for maintenance, transportation, and food services. Private contracts are sometimes more efficient and cost-effective.

Permanent Substitutes

Supplying schools with a position allocation for permanent substitutes supports many possibilities for improved school climate and indirect reduction of violence. Permanent substitutes are assigned to each school to substitute for teachers whenever they are out. They are a valuable resource because they know students and school policy. Tension in classrooms is reduced when the substitute is familiar with and to the students. Additionally, the quality of instruction is maintained when the teacher is absent.

On days when permanent substitutes are not in classrooms, they can be a valuable resource by relieving teachers for other activities. Teachers need opportunities during the school day to attend meetings with parents or to visit other classrooms to observe new teaching techniques.

The permanent substitutes can be an important link with the community. When the persons in this position are connected to the local community, they can be invaluable in coordinating the school volunteer program and in serving as an important information link.

Human Resource Services

Each district controls policies that have an impact on the job satisfaction of its employees. Job satisfaction can affect teacher or administrator performance that escalates or deescalates confrontation, anxiety, tension, and student achievement. Some suggested district procedures and policies include:

- Invest in an effective Employee Assistance Plan (EAP). Confidential counseling should be available for help with personal problems involving financial constraints, family crisis, chemical dependencies, and related difficulties.

- Design a center to assist teachers who are struggling with their pedagogical skills. The center provides help to teachers seeking improved skills. It also becomes a resource to principals who identify teachers in need of intensive professional help. Like the EAP, the center should be a confidential service in a helpful atmosphere. Small districts could examine the possibility of forming a consortium for such services. Local university programs in education may be a willing partner to such an effort.

- Establish easy leave policies. A year's leave should be given upon request, with no reason necessary. The only stipulations needed might be an agreement that a job within the system is guaranteed upon returning.
- Investigate 4-over-5 plans, where staff can have one fourth of their salary deducted for 4 years. Employees can take the fifth year off with pay.

Following reports of repeated verbal abuse of students, a frustrated, dissatisfied teacher was encouraged to attempt a career in another direction. A liberal leave policy, which functioned as a security blanket, made the administrator's tasks much less complicated. The teacher ventured into the retail world. A capable person found a more rewarding niche, and students who were suffering from her job mismatch were relieved.

A high school teacher took the 4-over-5 option to try a lifestyle in another part of the country. Teachers have taken the 4-over-5 option to attempt opening a business, have extended maternity leave, or attend graduate school. Some teachers, using the plan for forced savings, have taken the lump sum at the end of the 4 years to use toward retirement or children's college expenses. Whatever the outcome, job satisfaction is increased when frustrated teachers are presented with options.

With such leave possibilities, many employees never return. Disgruntled employees move on to other positions. Employees who do return are often refreshed and more convinced that education is where they should be. Benefits are directly experienced by students and the more positive climate created by a more satisfied teacher.

Crisis Response

During and after a crisis, the assistance that is provided by the district office is critical. Organized counseling assistance teams should be trained and on call to move rapidly into a school in crisis. For instance, if an unexpected or violent death occurs in the school community, the team should be available. A middle school child was abducted on her way to school. By the noon news, the community was aware of the situation. A crisis team moved into the school and remained for 5 days, until word was received that the student had been murdered. The team stayed for 1 week following the funeral to maintain grief groups and assist individuals.

Teams at each school should develop crisis plans for emergencies as probable as severe weather, or improbable as hostage taking. (Details are available in Chapter 8.) Teams from several schools with similar characteristics may be more effective in considering wider ranges of possibilities. A school located under a flight pattern has a contingency plan in case of a plane crash. Several scenarios of possible disasters have been anticipated. Staff are aware of their functions and responsibilities. A neighboring school has a coordinating plan if an evacuation is necessary. The district office should exhibit leadership in overseeing that all schools have developed crisis plans. Additionally, a communication plan should be centralized for coordination efforts.

Creating Equity for Tough Schools

The central office is especially challenged in a variety of ways with creating equity within tough schools. The label "tough school" does not imply a bad school. A tough school simply contains more challenges to providing the most suitable setting for learning. Many students come to school with several deficits working against their success. As young children, they may have had no one to model or expect complete sentences from their oral language. No one read to them, and there were no books in the home. They may have bad and painful teeth, or other physical needs are not met.

As they grow older, they may have to assume responsibility for care of younger children or parents who are dysfunctional. One middle school girl had the duty of staying out of sight in her father's car while it was parked at bars. She was there to drive him home when he passed out, so the family could get him to work the next day.

Cultural deprivation is often coupled with negative impressions about school. The home setting instills a mistrust of school because it is a place where the student's parents found no success. School is one more suspicious institution. The potential for violence is greater in tough schools because of these complicating factors.

Tough schools can be urban or rural. Tough schools usually do not have organized, politically astute, and connected parents who know how to play lobbying games. Equity for tough schools becomes a moral issue, with more time and money being required for education to be equal. Every school district has a variety of critical considerations for tough schools, which include:

- Being sure that the school receives equal care and quality of staff. Schools with less politically astute parents sometimes are targeted to receive leftover or substandard materials, maintenance, and teachers forced out of other schools.
- Recognizing and compensating the physical and emotional costs of those employees working in the most demanding schools. Employees in specified schools in Houston and other districts earn extra money. If possible, allow and provide for regular transfer of personnel in and out of tough schools.
- Reducing the pupil/teacher ratios in tough schools
- Maintaining high expectations for all schools

Final Thoughts

The support that the district office gives to schools and their leaders is essential in helping them establish a climate conducive to building school communities. Several configurations of school governance are presently evolving. The district as a service provider is central to the quality of all of the new relationships.

For Consideration

Reread the scenarios in Chapter 2. Consider what role the district office should play in each situation.

Safe School Facilities

Interviews with convicted criminals have revealed important information about the factors they used to select their victims. Criminals avoid attacking, robbing, and assaulting people who are assured, directed, and fit. Our school communities can also discourage harm by knowing where they are going, communicating their direction and successes, and by maintaining facilities that declare the school is cared for and tended.

Target hardening is the military term for achieving this stature:

> In its simplest form, target hardening is a security concept that significantly decreases, deters, or prevents crime against specific individuals or particular institutions. A soft target is an easy target; a hard target is a difficult one. Those who become target hardened are much less likely to become victims of crime. They are simply overlooked as potential victims. (Quarles, 1989, p. 12)

A range of target hardening strategies exists. Strategies extend from actions that are subtle to overtly and strongly communicating suppression of undesirable behavior. The best strategies for each school or district will be a combination unique to the individual situation and community.

Target Hardening Strategies

1. A clean, attractive school increases pride and discourages undesirable behavior.
2. Analysis of crime patterns leads to solutions.
3. Staff also need to feel safe and secure.
4. Access to the school needs to be restricted.
5. Hired security may be necessary.
6. Restrictions on student apparel can be important.

A Clean, Attractive School Increases Pride and Discourages Undesirable Behavior

A school with broken windows, graffiti, litter, broken furniture in the halls, and smelly, overflowing trash bins invites further ugliness. Years ago Walt Disney concluded that if litter is collected immediately, there is less litter to collect. People are more likely to leave litter if other litter exists. Similarly, graffiti is more likely to appear if other graffiti exists.

An orderly school will require less maintenance. More important, attractive schools are a source of pride to students and the community. A group consciousness develops to protect the school.

When planning new school construction, many districts are shedding institutional vestiges for designs more like professional centers. Linkages between school attractiveness and school pride relate to an overall attitude that benefits the school. Neat and orderly surroundings foster the same type of student behavior.

Hampton High School, a small high school in rural Tennessee, held a negative reputation in the surrounding area. Students were disruptive, attendance was dismal, and the dropout rate was disturbing. A new principal arrived with the central mission of changing the downward trends. Initial emphasis was placed on improving the facility. The forestry program, lead by an enthusiastic teacher, quickly became a source of visual and academic pride. Landscaping improved the outside appearance of the school, and the forestry team captured national ranking and distinction.

The principal involved other students in school improvement by assigning restrooms to different groups. Each sponsoring club received a small fund to use for the paint or decoration it selected. Randomly entering any restroom in the school will reveal neither a piece of paper on the floor nor a word on the wall. Involving the students in the improved appearance of the school produced a radical change in school climate. Because she changed the climate and downward spiral with these kinds of initiatives, the principal received a state award as an outstanding high school principal.

An area of hallway in a high school in Rockledge, Florida, was constructed with wallboard. Students felt compelled to put their fists through the wall as a symbol of manhood. Administrators quickly learned that the punched hole grew larger throughout the day. They framed a series of student-designed posters to be used as immediate cover for any hole that appeared. The problem quickly diminished.

As a newly assigned principal, I anxiously drove to my new school to catch first sight of it just before daylight. Approaching the campus, located on a major highway, I was struck with the impression created by the lone campus spotlight carefully lighting a dead tree. A place to begin was immediately apparent. Landscaping, flowers, an up-to-date clean marquee indicate care and tending. The curb appeal of the campus influences the overall perception of the school. Community projects for improvement of the outer school are also an easy way to get many community volunteers together. Landscaping projects are relaxed, and anyone with a shovel becomes an expert. Planning, planting, securing greenery, and maintaining landscaping are also positive opportunities for community members who thought they had nothing to contribute.

Because landscaping is so visible and tangible, finding sponsors is easier than with many other needs. Local businesses are easily interested in contributing to the project. Several environmental sources of grant funds support local initiatives to improve school appearance.

Schools with transient student populations especially need tree planting as a way to assist students to think in long-range terms. Commitment to the school is focused differently when there is interest in watching a small seedling become a mature tree. Individual classrooms can adopt particular trees for watering and care, or monitor certain campus areas. Landscaping projects furnish opportunities to model such concepts as commitment, legacy, and responsibility.

For a new principal, quick orientation to the facility leads to early efficient and effective behavior. The survey shown in Box 7.1 is worth an initial time commitment for a new principal. These key areas within the facility are related to smooth operation and a safer school environment. Even experienced principals can use the survey for a fresh review of their schools.

Analysis of Crime Patterns Leads to Solutions

Within improving schools, principals are continually analyzing basic data, gathering and evaluating patterns concerning attendance rates, tardiness, and graduation rates. Principals in exemplary schools extend analysis to other kinds of information. For instance, suspension and expulsion patterns contain answers and suggest questions. Examination of suspension and expulsion information can reveal changes in reasons for the behavior or changes in the students involved. For example, a sudden soaring of suspension rates for Japanese-American students may reinforce growing suspicion about a new gang being formed. If suspension rates for any segment of the school population exceed state and national percentages, there needs to be a close examination of the school curriculum and services.

Simple analysis of when and where criminal behavior exists on the school campus provides a focal point to reduce and eliminate it. If 30% of robberies are occurring because students are pulling gold jewelry from other students' necks in one hallway, approaches to changing this are quickly apparent. Increased hallway surveillance with personnel or cameras may be needed. An information campaign discouraging students from wearing expensive jewelry might also be appropriate.

Analysis requires data collection. Many software packages are available to make it possible to retrieve specific information quickly.

	BOX 7.1	

School Operations Survey

COMMENTS	✓	AREA FOR CHECKING
		Locate a school map to become familiar with physical characteristics of the plant.
		Survey safety of walking routes of students. Check crossing guard locations and schedules.
		Examine entrances for security. Consider the number of entrances that are absolutely necessary.
		Locate the following:
		a. boiler room
		b. major electrical panel and main shut-off switch
		c. heating and/or air-conditioning panels
		d. emergency power equipment
		e. storage areas
		f. water shut-off valves
		Locate blueprints of the school. Orient several other key people to the location of the blueprints.
		Periodically tour the plant with the lead custodian to determine his or her perspective about needs, problems, and security/safety factors.

BOX 7.1

(Continued)

COMMENTS	✓	AREA FOR CHECKING
		Review key inventory. Know the number and location of each master key. Consider database software for categorizing and accuracy of accounting.
		Learn how to unlock and lock all secured areas, including outside gates and fences.
		Identify locations of all trash bins. Is pick-up schedule timely, convenient, and considerate of student safety?
		Consider access and facility needs of physically challenged students, staff, and guests.
		Tour the plant on separate occasions to observe:
		a. security
		b. safety
		c. hiding possibilities
		d. flow patterns of students outside the building
		e. fence or boundary suitability
		Learn the procedures for requesting maintenance services and capital improvements. Analyze where the responsibility rests for making requests and also check the effectiveness of paper flow.

BOX 7.1

(Continued)

COMMENTS	✓	AREA FOR CHECKING
		With a staff committee, review or establish emergency evacuation plans and procedures. Be sure the plan includes an alternate site to which students could be relocated. Clarify responsibilities of key personnel in emergencies. Have traffic flow of emergency vehicles clearly decided. Know who will deal with media. (See other crisis plans guidelines in Chapter 8.)
		Review energy conservation plans and utilization printouts.
		Learn how to operate the security alarm system if one is installed in your building.
		Learn the names of personnel at the:
		a. police or sheriff's department
		b. fire department
		Make an appointment and meet with them.
		Review any past security problems with the lead custodian and local police.
		Locate and identify the safety of storage of all chemicals, cleaning supplies, and so on. Learn the system used to determine expiration dates and disposal of all chemicals.
		Examine the roof of the school for safety, needed repairs, and security.

BOX 7.1

(Continued)

COMMENTS	✓	AREA FOR CHECKING
		Be sure to assemble a small tool kit for your desk that includes a hammer, screwdriver, pliers, and so on.
		Review property inventories and procedures for filing, tagging, and processing new property. Be sure that responsibility for the security of all property is carefully assigned.
		Learn how to operate the fire alarm.
		Learn how to activate emergency shut-off to the alarm.
		Review fire alarm evacuation procedures.
		Review fire alarm records.
		Establish a fire alarm schedule. Plan for alternative times of the day, with access to some doors denied.
		Analyze traffic flow patterns around the school. Check clarity of directional signs. Separate bus and car traffic if possible.
		Analyze safety of student flow to buses and cars.
		Ride bus routes to learn your community and to have reference for accidents and bus stop problems. Consider any possibilities for improvement in routines.
		Analyze parking areas for safety, adequate lighting, clarity of directional signs.

BOX 7.1

(Continued)

COMMENTS	✓	AREA FOR CHECKING
		Check clarity of directional signs within and outside the building. Is the office easy to locate? Do all doors contain numbers or names?
		At night, check lighting outside and inside the building for safety and security.
		Learn to operate lighting for the building, stage, athletic facilities, and all outside areas.
		Examine location, conditions, and maintenance reports of any playground equipment.
		Learn the location of the public address system. Learn to operate it.
		Learn the location and operation of beeper systems, answering machines, intercom, and bullhorns.
		Identify locations of vending machines. Analyze possibilities of better locations. Know how to open them or who to contact to stock. Learn the stocking schedule. Find out who empties money from machines and how the money is handled. Locate and examine contracts regarding vending machines.
		Learn how to refill and perform simple procedures on all copy machines. Examine contracts on copiers. Analyze supply costs and sources of supplies.
		Analyze student flow within the cafeteria.

BOX 7.1

(Continued)

COMMENTS	✓	AREA FOR CHECKING
		Check for history of health department compliance.
		Tour cafeteria with the manager to discuss problems, security, safety, and needs.
		Examine delivery routes and schedules.
		Post in appropriate locations throughout the campus contact names for emergencies to include:
		a. fire department
		b. police department
		c. school district lines of command
		d. transportation
		e. district maintenance
		f. food service
		g. media
		h. copier repair

For instance, all staff and student cars should be required to have parking stickers, which make it possible to determine quickly if a vehicle does not belong on campus. Data should be filed regarding the make, model, color, tag number, and other pertinent information for immediate referral in case of an accident or other incident. Many schools record every entry and exit of vehicles for possible analysis and linkage to crimes. Combining student and faculty parking areas, creating curved access, prohibiting access to cars during the school day, and adding speed bumps all increase safety in outside areas.

Consider problems that are evident from the data collected in the sample in Box 7.2.

Changes in lighting, supervision, and scheduling patterns sometimes produce inexpensive solutions to problems. Involving students in finding solutions to school problems produces many benefits. Students' feelings of commitment to the school increase when they have a chance to participate and there is evidence that their opinion is respected. For many students, experience on an action team or a problem-solving committee may be unique; they might never before have had an opportunity to solve problems peacefully.

Solutions also are more likely to be viable when the solution arrives from a variety of sources close at hand. For example, students can produce workable models for better outdoor lighting for safer campus access in the evenings. Although, one California security director contends that a dark and silent night campus discourages entry, concomitantly saving utility costs (National School Safety Center, 1990).

A junior high in California photographs all gang graffiti for analysis and to use in increasing staff awareness of symbols and activity. Cameras and video cameras can provide useful data for gathering information. Photographs of vandalized areas and graffiti may add information that can be used in the process of determining a solution. They can be shown to witnesses to verify information. Photos can quickly be interpreted by faxing them to experts on esoteric fringe groups, such as Satanic cults or newly emerging hate gangs.

Some districts feel that awareness is essential at a local level. They send representatives for training in specifics about gang formation

BOX 7.2

Data Collection

	LOCATION				
Offenses	**Wing A**	**Library**	**Auditorium**	**Room 23**	**Room 24**
Theft	II	I		III	II
Fighting	III	I	III	I	I
Vandalism	I	II	I	I	I
Harassment		II	IIIII		
Vulgarity		I	IIII	I	

and occult behavior to institutes like NASSP's aptly titled "Streets and Schools: Kids, Gangs, Guns."

Portland areas schools have access to computer linkages that supply rapid information regarding gang member movement (Prophet, 1990). As school officials and police know, closing a crack house or clamping down on an apartment area full of drug dealing will only force those involved to move to another location, at least for a while. Forewarning administrators in other attendance areas can assist them in admission and enrollment decisions. Police statistics can help new principals learn patterns of crime in each school attendance area. Eventually, school administrators will know that a drug raid in one area means an increase in enrollment and gang activity in a neighboring school.

A quick reading of the newspaper indicates changes and potentially tense times within a school. Headlines regarding a drive-by shooting, or a story about arson in a certain neighborhood, alert principals to a potential response within the school setting. Aware school leaders are prepared with "buttondown" strategies. When tension escalated, our staff was given the "buttondown" code. Time between classes and for lunch was reduced. Small privileges were removed. The number of highly visible adults throughout the campus increased. To heighten their visibility, male staff members were released from some classes during lunch periods.

It is also useful if there are agreements with neighboring schools to have administrators on call for one another in an exceptional instance. A middle school student maintained that she was raped by a construction worker on our campus. After having sex with another student at her home, she was terrified that she was pregnant. Two days of investigation were required to clarify what had happened. In the meantime, rumors exploded in the small community and horror stories with racial overtones abounded. A rumor hot line was established. The high school principal called and offered to make his personnel available on campus to demonstrate a secure atmosphere. We gladly accepted. With extra assistance and rapid information dissemination, we were able to calm fears by the end of the week.

On one occasion I sent a letter to parents, explaining that recent student behavior was increasingly unacceptable and was going to result in certain campus restrictions. With the letter to parents in the mail, I addressed our 3,000 students to explain that until improvements were noted, many new restrictions would apply. Lunch periods were shortened. Groups were not allowed to gather. Time between classes was reduced. Soda machines were sealed. Evening events were canceled.

This resulted in a brief protest and walkout of 40 students the next morning. When asked, all but 7 returned to campus for the morning bell. The following morning there was a a walkout of hundreds of students, chanting and carrying banners supporting the school. Strong support for our stand also came from parents. We received letters, telephone calls, and positive reactions from parents during media interviews. Some parents even arrived on campus before and after school and during lunch to demonstrate their support by supplying additional adult presence.

Within a few days, behavior improved, tensions were reduced, and schedules returned to normal. The discomfort of rescheduling, listening to student complaints, and tightening student movement throughout the campus was well worth increased community and student understanding of the level of expected behavior within our school.

Another aspect of crime pattern analysis involves determining the locations of violence on the campus. Often more violent behavior is concentrated in certain teachers' classrooms. For a graduate research project, an assistant principal analyzed discipline referral patterns in her large high school. She began by asking the six school administrators to list independently the school's five weakest academically performing teachers. Though in a variety of orders, all six administrators named the same five teachers. An analysis of discipline referrals identified that those five teachers also accounted for 62% of discipline referrals. In a similar study, a school security chief found that in one school 3% of the staff were responsible for 50% of the referrals (Stover, 1988). These same startling figures could probably be found in most schools. Disruptive student behavior is more likely to occur in badly organized, unchallenging classrooms.

A few teachers often lack good instructional skills, resulting in disconnected students with too much time. When the students rebel, the teachers lack strategies for handling the situation, and then disruption escalates. Again, approaches to solving the problem are apparent. These teachers need intense training to improve their academic performances and to supply them with classroom management techniques. Pointing at or moving in front of a student may be the fuse to detonate physically aggressive behavior. Training teachers to make nonthreatening statements and exhibit correct nonverbal behavior toward students can reduce problems.

Teachers should be trained in specific modes of behavior in case they encounter students fighting or a student with a weapon. Tone of voice and choice of words are critical in defusing potential violence. I remember the lesson I learned when I asked a student to produce the weapon she had tucked into her waistband. She promptly exhibited a gun and pointed it at me. I then asked her to place it on a nearby table, which was the request I should have made in the beginning of the encounter. The correct request would have resulted in provoking a less escalated choice on her part and would have avoided a stress test for me.

Professional development centers, offering support and detailed assistance for teachers' academic difficulties, are becoming available in districts or through consortia among districts. If teaching performance and technique do not improve after a carefully developed improvement plan has been attempted, the teacher should be removed. Both direct and indirect welfare of many children depend on it.

Staff Also Need to Feel Safe and Secure

Staff members need to feel safe in their work setting. Adequate lighting, reasonable security measures, and easy communication links contribute to that feeling. School leadership may have to remind staff members about commonsense safety precautions. Many dedicated teachers become so involved in their projects that they are the only person left in a wing of the school or in the auditorium. Reminders about safe procedures are routinely needed, and training is also important. Local police agencies often have programs available to train citizens in crime prevention behavior and self-defense strategies.

A committee of staff members can effectively inspect a facility to consider ways to make it safer for everyone. Gathering ideas from a wider perspective increases the degree of awareness of safe procedures. Staff members should be discouraged from working within the building alone, at any time and in any setting. Staggered shifts of custodial assistance may provide better services while also lengthening safe hours of access to the building.

Glass doors or panels in walls can increase visibility for staff members. Conference rooms for meetings with parents and students are often settings for tense encounters. Shatterproof glass in doors or in walls increases the feeling of security for counselors and teachers during meetings with volatile parents or students.

All teachers should have access to interlinked computers, giving them immediate contact for assistance in a classroom. This type of technology provides instant and confidential communication. Silent buzzers to summon support may be useful in some settings.

Access to the School Needs to Be Limited

To minimize the possibilities of strangers entering the campus, restrict access to the school to a minimal number of doors. Entrances and driveways should be visible to office personnel. Front windows must be clear of obstructions, so that streets and traffic in front are visible to personnel. Posted signs should welcome visitors and request that they check in at the main office.

Some schools may require closed-circuit monitoring to increase security. Smaller plants or carefully trimmed trees that prevent hidden spaces are good ideas for landscaping around the school. Schools in San Diego, California, are gradually replacing chain-link fences with ornamental wrought iron (National School Safety Center, 1990). This sturdier, more secure addition also adds to the attractiveness of the campus.

Visitor passes should be issued to all guests. Staff will need to be assisted in developing their comfort level to issue a friendly challenge to persons in the school whom they cannot readily identify. Parents will not be offended but relieved at vigilant efforts to assure their children's security within the school setting.

Random surveys of parking areas by school personnel are also important in promoting a safe campus. During routine scans, I have encountered students necking in cars, weapons in backseats, students in tears for a variety of reasons, a private investigator watching a house across the street from the school, a teacher's car being towed for back payments, a father without legal custody watching for his son, and a car flying in reverse through the parking lot. (A 4-year-old left in the car had crawled under the steering wheel.) A rapid walk through parking areas is essential on a regular basis. Such practices are all part of the principal's objective of being a very visible leader.

In some schools guarded entrances might need to be equipped with metal detectors and might also need to contain security cameras. Metal detectors sell for about $10,000 each and are in use in several urban school systems. Hand-held wand metal detectors are also randomly used for potentially volatile after-school events (Harrington-Lueker, 1992b).

Because estimates of annual crime and vandalism costs in schools run from $50 million to $600 million (Greenbaum & Turner, 1989), principals are utilizing every technological security technique known. Special door combinations, alarm systems, motion detectors, infrared sensors to detect body temperatures, and other such gadgetry, once found only in espionage movies, are making their way into school inventories. In some districts these devices are reducing the extensive property losses each year. As the school is viewed as a hardened target, breaking-and-entering rates come down. Philadelphia Public Schools have added on-line intrusion alarm systems throughout their buildings. Key codes designate who can enter; and daily printouts identify every entry that takes place. None of these high-tech approaches is perfect at keeping all weapons and criminals out of the school, but they can all provide powerful deterrence in some settings.

Roof access should be evaluated. Remove garbage bins next to the building. Examine drainpipes and window overhangs for their assistance in scaling walls. Survey any other elevated areas surrounding the school campus.

We found owners of neighboring property to be cooperative in assisting our school security efforts. On one occasion, our school received a positive response to a letter we sent to an out-of-state real estate firm, requesting that the large land parcel they managed behind our school be cleaned and cleared of brush. The area had become very overgrown and was full of mattresses that vagrants used as a place to sleep. For a few months, there had been several incidents of classroom televisions being stolen, and the kitchen had been robbed. Some students also liked to take a shortcut through that field, which was littered with drug paraphernalia. Following cleanup, our vandalism ended. Commonly, property owners are willing to assist, not only because it is the right thing to do but also because schools' reputations as safe enhance their property values.

Access to unsupervised areas within the building also must be reviewed. Stairwells, stage areas, custodial supply closets, electrical or furnace rooms, and other largely deserted areas need to be evaluated for safety and security. Hiding places can be blocked or carefully secured. Simple convex mirrors or increased lighting can highlight blind spots and may enhance safety as much as security.

Hired Security May Be Necessary

A guard at the front entrance of the school can be a hindrance to some violent and criminal elements. New York City Schools spend more than $43 million a year on a security staff of 2,050, and Los

Angeles Schools employ 310, with an $18.3 million budget (Stover, 1988). Security guards are often a deterrent to the extensive costs incurred annually because of vandalism and theft in schools.

For greatest efficiency and safety, there needs to be planning when security guards or off-duty police are hired for specific after-school activities. When the principal supplies campus maps for use by officers, they are more likely to be able to construct plans for movement patterns. Plans for before, during, and after the event as well as contingency plans should be designed. Officers should be skilled at moving and funneling large crowds in peaceful, nonthreatening ways.

Having uniformed officers regularly on campus is a delicate issue. "The use of uniformed police in schools may alienate or antagonize some students and make the school seem like an armed camp" (Rich, 1992, p. 38). When the presence of police officers is tied to the curriculum, the intimidation that can result is reduced. Officers sometimes conduct drug awareness, safety, physical fitness, or first aid training sessions for students. They can lead field trips to courts and prisons as part of the political science curriculum.

Various programs call for an officer to be in a school from one day a week to full time. When I was the principal in one school setting, it was my good fortune that an officer, who was conducting drug awareness training, was present when several unfortunate incidents occurred at the school. During her one-day-a-week stay, she arrested people in my office on two different occasions, assisted me in dispersing two volatile marital disputes in the parking lot, transported a student home following his father's suicide, and supervised the aftermath of a tragic car accident in front of our school that resulted in a fatality. She was also an important communication link in other instances when I needed a contact in the police department for information. Her assistance was invaluable.

Legalities involved with placing police officers in schools have been examined. Frisby and Beckham (1993) reported in the *NASSP Bulletin* that "in some settings, the potential for violence justifies the regular presence of a law enforcement officer" (p. 10). Police officers are highly trained in knowing legal precedents of acceptable and appropriate levels of response in meeting student resistance. The training and expertise of any hired or district-employed guards must be carefully examined from a prudent legal standpoint.

Selection of the suitable combination of deterrents requires careful assessment of their appropriateness to the individual setting.

Restrictions on Student Apparel Can Be Important

Gang and drug situations often call for stricter measures regarding acceptable student clothing and possessions. Some schools restrict student clothing that depicts gang affiliation: "Wearing colors" is prohibited.

Restrictions may include items like attache cases, beepers, and cellular phones that are commonly used for drug deals. Some high schools' policies have required clear plastic carriers and eliminated book bags and purses. Hats are often restricted because of gang affiliation and the use of the hatband for concealing weapons. Banning hats and restricting clothing such as strap T-shirts and gang colors also helps identify strangers on campus. Federal initiatives vigorously support most efforts to suppress drugs and the presence of weapons in schools. Convictions for possessing firearms on school campuses can carry a 5-year prison sentence, with a $5,000 fine (Harrington-Lueker, 1992a).

Detroit City Schools banned certain expensive labeled clothing, leather jackets, and gold jewelry (Landen, 1992). Peer pressure to wear labels can increase thefts and absenteeism if a student is not able to conform to the accepted trend. Baltimore City Schools and other areas of the country are promoting school uniforms as a way to reduce aggressive acts among students (Landen, 1992). A junior high principal in Maryland observed an increase in honor roll membership, and another noted a decrease in fighting between students after uniforms were mandated (LaPoint, Holloman, & Alleyne, 1992). When his school began requiring uniforms, a Washington, DC, principal established business partnerships to secure donated uniforms for economically struggling families.

Because of difficulties with concealing weapons and drugs, some schools have even removed lockers. Alex Rascon, who directed security for San Diego schools, reported that removing lockers reduced fights that often occurred around lockers. Student punctuality in reporting to class also improved (Ordovensky, 1993). Where they still exist, lockers are school property and random searches are legal. The

reasonable suspicion standard has extended search possibilities. Regardless, legalities involving all types of searches need to be refer-
enced to local court rulings.

Final Thoughts

School officials are continually challenged with designing schools
that are safe from intruders and yet are warm and welcoming to
students and the general community. "Metal detectors, drug and
weapon-sniffing dogs, security personnel, and restricted rules and
regulations are not solutions—they are techniques to handle the problem on an ad hoc basis" (Landen, 1992, p. 4). To meet the needs of each
school setting for a safe and orderly environment, the effects of these
extreme measures must be assessed.

Planning for and Dealing
With the Worst-Case Scenarios

Though concerted effort has been made to create a positive, nurturing school climate, violence and disaster can erupt. Every school and school district needs to develop plans for a variety of worst-case scenarios. Worst-case situations can be organized around these three themes:

- Purposeful, human-caused disasters: for example, murder, hostage taking, bombing
- Accidental disasters: for example, chemical spills, some fires, transportation accidents, malfunctioning equipment
- Natural disasters: for example, tornadoes, hurricanes, earthquakes, some fires

The extent of damage can often be reduced by careful approaches. A three-pronged effort should involve:

- Schoolwide and district planning for any contingency
- Training staff to anticipate necessary actions during a variety of disasters
- Training students to react to a disaster

Schoolwide and
District Planning for Any Contingency

Planning for disaster is essential to reduce danger to students and staff. Confidently addressing a crisis with direction in mind determines the difference between panicky delays and calm, calculated action. It takes a conscientious commitment to design comprehensive planning that includes routine review, update, and orientation.

Each school's plan will be distinct in its consideration of geography, problematic possibilities, and other unique features. Rural, isolated schools are challenged by the distance police and medical services have to come. Traffic congestion around urban schools may cause delays in critical medical services. Distinctive features of each school dictate the particulars for sound planning.

Attention in the media to tragedies elsewhere in the country sometimes spawns copycat violence. It is prudent to examine one's campus with an eye toward potential danger from such violence. Following the Stockton, California, playground killings, we examined our campus with a new focus. After selecting high points where a sniper could perch, we moved our physical education activities to the back of the school. This removed large numbers of students from sight of an expressway overpass adjoining our school. Most local police departments have specially trained units willing to walk the campus and adjoining areas to offer other points for consideration. Access to major highways, proximity to airports, railways, chemical plants, and other hazards requires specific alternatives. Plans formed within each school must dovetail with comprehensive district planning.

Such crucial planning must include a variety of stakeholders. The principal must carefully involve wide representation in developing contingencies. This assures that broader possibilities are considered, and it also enhances the probability that the plan's importance will be communicated to an extended audience of those involved. Within a school, the planning committee should include administrators, teachers, parents, custodians, special education teachers, bus drivers, community members, representatives from neighboring schools or evacuation areas, and, for selected sessions, students. A school district representative is needed as a liaison.

Specialists consulted for specific suggestions in planning should include representatives from the telephone company, emergency medical teams, and the police department.

There are many guidebooks that provide assistance and recommendations for specific situations. For instance, the National Education Association published guidelines developed by Chester Quarles (1989), with details for handling robbery, rape, and hostage taking situations. Districts and schools are receptive to sharing their planning efforts with other schools.

Ideally consortia within geographic areas would meet to critique and expand crisis plans and to outline commitments of resources in the event of a tragedy. For instance, the number of competent counselors in a district is inadequate to meet the needs generated in a crisis. Pooling personnel and other resources would strengthen the quality of the response within any district in the consortium.

Elements of a Crisis Plan

1. Communications
2. Outline responsibilities
3. Establish the command center
4. Evacuation routes

Communications

How many principals have occasionally yearned for the busy telephone to stop ringing, for a moment of peace in the school day? Yet, in an emergency, the telephone becomes a life link. Precise and regularly updated telephone chains need to be established.

Emphasis on saving lives is the primary concern in any crisis. Medical assistance numbers are most imperative. Clear references need to be made for a variety of types of medical assistance. If someone is trapped in debris, which number is called first? If someone is shot, which number best applies? Law enforcement and school district office contacts also should lead the list. Access to an assortment of numbers in these key sites will assure quick contact. A private, unpublished line needs to be available into each school and to the district office to assure immediate access in case of an emergency.

After being notified, trained personnel in the district office should handle all other calls. Activities in the school will prescribe that time and personnel be used for more critical needs. District calls might include:

- notice to other schools for backup personnel or evacuation information
- notice to alternative locations
- coordination of transportation
- notification of parents and spouses
- alerts to utility company officials for special services (i.e., mobile phone banks)
- dispatching district personnel for specific service
- information to a radio station willing to be used as a communications link
- other media
- location and dispatching of vital equipment and data

During a protracted crisis, written statements placed by each phone help assure that identical messages are given by any staff member who may be responding.

If a perpetrator or natural disaster eliminates telephone service, what are the alternatives in your setting? Fax services would be affected by telephone disruption. A cellular telephone is indispensable, but if one is not available, car phones may serve the purpose. Consider technological links that are not affected by telephone lines.

Computer access to outside sources and straight to emergency sources is possible. In some settings, ham radio could be the only communication. The planning team should brainstorm possibilities for alternative communication.

Other Communication Issues. Inside the school, the intercom allows immediate communication to all areas. Rapid instructions are often necessary to save lives. Intercoms must be established in kitchen areas and other nonclassroom settings. Portable classrooms must be equally served. A few carefully designed codes can transmit a message to teachers to seal the room, to cover windows, or to evacuate.

Parents must be aware of alternative plans and should know what radio station to consult for directions. Parent traffic and panic can impair medical service access. Plans for moving parents to a large area for instructions or to wait for information are beneficial. Carefully selected personnel would be assigned duties to move people to central points.

If many students are injured, carefully compiled information is essential. Students might have to be evacuated to several medical centers. A school representative should be dispatched to each location. The principal must know who is being transported to each facility. Accurate information is essential. Identification of bodies may be a difficult task required of teachers. Most appropriately, the principal will be designated as the person to inform parents of injuries or deaths.

Outline Responsibilities

A chain of command must be considered. If the principal were injured or taken hostage, who are the next two or three people who would take charge? What information must they have?

Other responsibilities require clear designation: Who makes initial telephone calls? Who moves children? Who handles the media? Keep in mind that media may be banned from school property to spare parents or staff painful questions. In most situations, media and parents should be separated. Where will suspects be detained or questioned? Does designating the campus into quadrants of responsibility make sense? What are the other roles that must be maintained?

Who manages traffic control inside and outside the building? A graduate student, serving as an administrative intern in a high school, was present when a shooting frenzy began in a hallway between classes. Three students were shot by another student. The parking lot turned into chaos, with students running for their cars and parents arriving from the neighborhood. Emergency vehicles lost valuable time in reaching the victims because of the traffic congestion. The intern bounded into the mayhem, effectively clearing lanes for ambulance access.

Many medical emergencies require helicopter access. Where on campus can a helicopter land without becoming entangled in overhead wires? How will the school communicate or mark this access for helicopter landing?

During an emergency, community members may be needed to supervise students and to help with other critical areas. Having a small group of specially selected and trained persons from the immediate area may prove to be a valuable resource. Lists of parents with police or medical expertise might be useful.

Establish the Command Center

A central area must be established as a command center. The main office of the school is most common, though alternative sites must be anticipated and designated.

The command center should contain a variety of items including:

- blueprints of the school
- bullhorns, walkie-talkies, bells, fresh batteries (Remember that two-way radios cannot be used if there is a bomb threat.)
- maps with established evacuation routes
- telephone lists, including unlisted telephone numbers for the central office
- a master key
- a register of all student names and addresses

These components should be easy to access and contained in a portable carrier for rapid transportation if necessary. With time and resources permitting, a command center would be even more efficiently supported if it included:

- a database of all student names and locations
- an automatic-dialing telephone system, often used for homework hotlines, to use for notifying parents
- a television
- markers and a board
- a fax machine

Evacuation Routes

In many crisis situations, all students and staff must be moved to an alternate location. Clear monitoring assignments should be established for personnel, with backups to cover absences. Maps with alternate routes should be available even though all personnel should practice walking a variety of routes.

Consider setting up checkpoints along the routes. Teachers must instinctively grab their roll books as they leave the classroom, to assist in accounting for each student in any emergency. This becomes critical in many situations. Roll books become the check system to identify children as they are picked up by parents. They can become the critical record to know exactly how many children may be held hostage or are missing.

Many large school systems maintain comprehensive crisis plans and are willing to supply copies to other districts. A written validated plan increases the confidence of personnel working within a crisis. Cultice (1992) noted that a written plan "adds dignity to the school district's crisis intervention efforts, assists in the utilization of available personnel, prevents impulsive decisions under pressures, conserves staff time and energy, improves staff morale, and promotes good public relations" (p. 69). The understanding and the links that are developed through training and planning benefit the school and the community. The principal is key to initiating these links.

Training Staff to
Anticipate a Variety of Disasters

When the details of establishing a crisis plan are considered, the critical nature of staff training is obvious. Staff members must be part of planning at all stages. Training also must be repeated and enhanced at regular intervals. Well-informed staff reduce feelings of helplessness and lack of control that often impede effective reaction to a crisis.

Staff development programs should contain opportunities for everyone to receive cardiopulmonary resuscitation (CPR) training and first aid instruction. The staff of each school should have several persons proficient in emergency medical procedures and CPR. For immediate reference, the list of trained personnel should be posted in a variety of areas throughout the campus. Having well-trained, informed personnel increases the probability of a confident approach if an emergency occurs. Confidence that a plan is in place, and that personnel are adequately trained and informed, helps prevent panicky behavior and delayed reaction. Addressing and rectifying the problem at hand can begin much more quickly.

Training Students to React to a Disaster

Regular drills in procedure are important if students are to respond effectively to an emergency. Drills should comply with local and state policies concerning fire and storm precautions. Students will do a better job of quick thinking and problem solving if their everyday routine is disturbed regularly. Every fire drill can be used to introduce a different variable. For example, a regularly used stairway or hallway can be blocked with a large sign, declaring "Fire ahead. Find another way out." One principal had a cardboard picture of a fire that she routinely placed in a regular evacuation route. Drills should also be practiced during lunchtime, with a full cafeteria.

Duck-and-cover drills within the classroom teach students to avoid window areas and to listen to a trusted adult in an emergency. Developing students who think and make quick reactions to unanticipated situations could save lives sometime in the future.

Planning for Healing After a Tragedy

Following a traumatic event, staff and students may experience a variety of feelings. Depending upon the experience, people who survive a tragedy will feel a range of extreme emotions, including anger, continued fear, grief, and guilt. Difficulty sleeping and eating are common. Flashbacks filled with dread and panic may even occur during the day.

Immediate and sustained counseling assistance following emergency events is essential. Many school districts have proactively developed teams of counselors and psychologists within the area to be on call for quick access if an emergency arises. These teams may be helpful for grief counseling at the sudden loss of a teacher or student.

Group counseling may be needed, or teachers can assist classes in discussing their reactions and feelings. Several books carefully cover death and dying and may prove to be therapeutic for classroom reading and discussion. Student reactions to catastrophe will differ greatly, depending on the following variables:

- age of the student
- emotional support system available in the family
- actually witnessing the shooting or violence against others
- whether the student has been a victim of previous violence

Play therapy for young students and art for any age can provide vehicles for expressing fears, anger, guilt, pain. Pynoos and Nader (1988) provide a useful resource by producing lists of student response to trauma and appropriate support systems for a variety of age ranges.

Victim advocates can reassure with credibility. They are especially important to assist healing for victims of sex crimes. A high school in Brooklyn, New York, maintains grieving rooms with counselors throughout the day (Flax, 1992). Violence is so prevalent in the neighborhood that staff and students cannot adequately recuperate before another student is killed. Ongoing counseling has become a basic service.

The school becomes the natural center for counseling for affected families. When community members are reluctant to go to the school, counseling should be offered at sites within the neighborhoods. Around-the-clock counseling hotlines also would serve persons suffering a fitful night.

Staff members will often immediately begin assisting others. Their grieving may be delayed while caring for others. Staff may especially appreciate care extended for completing worker's compensation forms, legal records, insurance claims, and other paper details. Principals need to be observant of staff behavior. Following the unexpected death of a first grader, the teacher responded with great professionalism to support the grief of the child's classmates. On the third day following the death, I sent the teacher home when he was finally assured that the students would be well cared for by our counselor and permanent substitute. He had been unable to express any emotion for fear of disturbing his students.

Likewise, district personnel need to safeguard the principal during severe stress and physical demand. Informal national networks of principals who have survived tragedy have been formed. During the spring of 1993, following several stressful months of pulling their communities and schools back from the devastation of Hurricane Andrew, I met a large delegation of principals from the Miami area at a conference in Sitka, Alaska. "Transforming Schools into Learning Communities" was the theme of the conference. The positive, committed spirit of the participants, the exceptional natural surroundings, and the content and format of the conference presented an optimum opportunity for healing and renewal. School officials need to be sure that these opportunities are available for administrators who experience life-or-death challenges.

The school should reopen as rapidly as possible following a tragic event. A wing or classroom where damage occurred may need to be sealed. Quick return helps healing begin. Patricia Busher, principal of Cleveland Elementary School in Stockton, California, maintains that any delay in reopening the school after Patrick Purdy killed five children on the playground with an assault rifle would have allowed deeper shock to set in (Smith, 1989). Busher stated, "I think that had the school closed, a day of shock would have set in and some people would have been virtually crippled and lost the power ever to return" (Smith, 1989, p. 10). Maintenance crews worked through the night, repairing walls and cleaning away evidence of the day's tragedy.

Occurrences must be clearly chronicled. This may be essential if any legal action is taken. For increased detail and accuracy, accounts should be compiled as quickly as possible after any incident. Independent accounts by many people will help clarify activities in the middle of much confusion. Anecdotal data are useful for learning how to design plans and take more efficient action if a similar tragedy should ever occur again. The written account may also be an important catharsis for some people.

Fund drives to erect memorials or to plant a tree in tribute to a victim are often therapeutic. In one school, students organized a parade protesting violence. Through such efforts, students can feel that they are helping in some way. The anniversary of the tragedy may warrant a tribute or ceremony. Healing is a complex process requiring extended time.

Final Thoughts

In 1940 a school's largest concerns included infractions involving gum chewing, talking, running in the building, and littering (Wheeler, 1989). Because societal demands for and concerns within schools have escalated, proactive leadership provided by the principal is essential to keep schools safe.

Careful planning and training are imperative to assist any school or district to more effectively handle any crisis. Extensively detailed assignment lists and communication contingencies will support rational responses, rather than panicked approaches to critical situations.

Healing within the community and school can be expedited when specially selected and trained teams are available. Time for recovery will vary with the individual. Similarly, time for the school community to recover will vary. Plans to deal with critical incidents must be individualized for each school setting and with the uniqueness of every crisis.

Commitment and courage are central ingredients for the principal to successfully reduce the potential for violence while simultaneously building a strong school culture for learning to take place. Courage is needed to continually challenge the many factors that work against a safe school. Commitment is needed to combat the more subtle forces that harm schools, such as politics, apathy, and stagnation. The school principal is the pivotal catalyst in making a difference.

Resource A

NEWS

for more information contact lew armistead (703)860-0200, ext. 233

FOR RELEASE 9:30 A.M. (EST), WEDNESDAY, MARCH 2

NASSP CALLS FOR 'WAR ON HANDGUNS AND OTHER WEAPONS'—MAILS 'CONTRACT' TO ALL U.S. SCHOOLS

WASHINGTON (DC) -- Secondary schools, parents, and students throughout the nation today were called upon to join a War on handguns and Other Weapons by the nation's largest school leadership organization.

"Today America is killing its kids," said Dr. Timothy J. Dyer, executive director, National Association of Secondary School Principals (NASSP). "There's no other way to describe this senseless American tragedy."

NASSP, which represents more than 40,000 school leaders, today is mailing a contract to all middle level and high schools in the United States. The contract provides specific, practical actions for students, parents, and the school to take in hopes of eliminating guns and other weapons from schools.

For example, students are asked not to bring weapons to school and to report handguns if they see them at school. Schools are called upon to provide an anonymous means of reporting handguns.

"This senseless violence is not a large city or small city problem," said Dyer. "It's not an urban or suburban problem. It's not a white, black or brown problem. The killing of our children is an American tragedy."

At a news conference today to announce the mailing of the contract, Dyer reported that 3,274 children under 19 years of age were murdered with guns in 1991. He also cited recent instances in Wisconsin and Michigan where an associate principal and a school superintendent, respectively, were shot and killed.

"There's no other way to describe this than an epidemic of death," said Dyer. "If an army from another country came into the United States and murdered 3,274 of our young people, we would instantly declare a state of war against that country. When we do it to ourselves, too many people simply look the other way. Now is the time for all of us to join the War on Handguns and Other Weapons."

Dyer also indicated that NASSP will develop partnerships with other organizations such as the Center to Prevent Handgun Violence to develop training materials which schools can use to prevent violence.

"Too many children today are repeatedly sent the message that guns are the answer to life's problems," said Sarah Brady, chair of the Center to Prevent Handgun Violence, who participated in today's news event. "As adults, we must set examples for our kids about ways to respond to emotions appropriately -- non-violently. Today's announcement by the NASSP encouraging parents and students to pledge to reduce gun violence is a tremendous step toward that goal."

Dyer asked that principals across the land encourage students and parents to sign the contract, along with themselves as representative of the school, as a way to promote actions which can help curtail the use of handguns and other weapons.

"Clearly, killing, violence, handguns, and other weapons are not the responsibility of just schools," Dyer said. "Educators do not teach students to shoot each other. I do not know of a single school that teaches a course called Killing 101."

However, he urged schools to adapt and use the contract to "call attention to the problem and to steps each and every one of us can take."

He also indicated that he did not expect using the contract would eliminate the problem. But he called the contract a step forward in the War Against Handguns and Other Weapons.

"For anyone to say this action is not worthy because it will not eliminate the problem is a total cop-out," Dyer charged. "Such an attitude is part of the problem which is killing our youth."

Dyer compared handgun violence in the United States with that in other nations. He reported that in 1990 handguns were used to kill 22 people in Great Britain, 13 in Sweden, 91 in Switzerland, 87 in Japan, 10 in Australia, 68 in Canada, and 10,567 in the United States.

-30-

Resource B

NATIONAL ASSOCIATION OF SECONDARY SCHOOL PRINCIPALS
STATEMENT OF POSITION

Weapons in Schools

Whereas, students have a right to attend school without a fear of weapons' violence to themselves or others;

Whereas, safe schools enhance the learning environment, necessary for quality schools which are essential to a successful democracy;

Whereas, the causes for violence are multiple: chronic poverty, the lack of jobs and role models, the disintegration of families, the loss of moral values, and a popular culture that seems to glorify violence at every turn;

Whereas, a major 1993 Louis Harris poll about guns among American youth reports that 1 in 25 students have taken a handgun to school in a single month, and 59 percent know where to get a handgun if they need one;

Whereas, violence is exacerbated with the increase of weapons in our schools resulting in some 31 deaths from guns during the 1992–93 school year; be it therefore known that,

the National Association of Secondary School Principals:

- supports passage of the Brady Bill which requires a waiting period and background check before legal purchase of a handgun;
- urges full enforcement of the Gun-Free School Zones Act of 1990;
- calls on Congress to pass the Safe Schools Act of 1993, with an amendment that will ban the purchase of a handgun and semi-automatic guns for any person under the age of 21;
- urges schools to provide staff training for weapons situations arising in school, and to implement student awareness programs which challenge youths' falsely held beliefs that they are invincible;
- challenges schools to implement apprehension, prevention, intervention, and counseling programs to combat possession of weapons and violent acts;
- encourages school-based parent involvement programs to include violence prevention strategies that emphasize the issue of easy access to handguns;
- exhorts school districts to establish violence prevention curriculum, grades K–12, and promote articulation among levels to ensure continuity in policies and practices;
- challenges Schools of Education to add conflict resolution and violence coping skills to their teacher preparation programs.

*Where principals appear in this statement, it refers also to assistant principals, vice principals, and deans (where the role is that of administrative support to the principal).

119

Resource C

Violence in the Media and Entertainment Industry

Whereas, in 1979, the National Association of Secondary School Principals urged the broadcasting and motion picture industries to work with educators and parents in moving toward a significant reduction of violent acts in television and film programming;

Whereas, the nation is experiencing an unrivaled period of juvenile violent crime perpetrated by youths from all races, social classes, and lifestyles;

Whereas, the average American child views 8,000 murders and 100,000 acts of violence on TV before finishing elementary school, and by the age of 18, that same teenager will have witnessed 200,000 acts of violence on TV, including 40,000 murders; and,

Whereas, the entertainment industry (movies, records, music videos, radio, and television) plays an important role in fostering anti-social behavior by promoting instant gratification, glorifying casual sex, encouraging the use of profanity, nudity, violence, killing, and racial and sexual stereotyping; be it therefore known that,

The National Association of Secondary School Principals:

- appreciates the efforts of the U.S. Attorney General to focus on the problem increasing violence in the media;

- stands in opposition to violence and insensitive behavior and dialogue in the entertainment industry;

- commends television broadcasters who have begun self-regulation by labeling each program it deems potentially offensive with the following warning: DUE TO VIOLENT CONTENT, PARENTAL DISCRETION IS ADVISED; and producers of music videos and records who use similar labeling systems;

- encourages parents to responsibly monitor and control the viewing and listening habits of their children with popular media products (records, videos, TV programs, etc.);

- calls upon advertisers to take responsible steps to screen the programs they support on the basis of their violent and profane content;

- supports federal legislation designed to decrease and monitor TV violence including:
  a. H.R. 288, sponsored by Representative Edwin Markey (MA) and Jack Fields (TX), requiring TVs to be equipped with a V-chip, enabling viewers to completely block programs classified as violent by the networks;
  b. S. 942, sponsored by David Durenburger (MN), requiring the Federal Communications Commission (FCC) to develop and codify standards to reduce TV violence; and

- calls upon the Federal Communications Commission to initiate hearings on violence in the media, and to consider as part of those hearings the establishment of guidelines for broadcasters to follow during prime time and children's viewing hours; furthermore, the FCC should use its licensing powers to ensure broadcasters' compliance with guidelines on violence and establish a strict procedure to levy fines against those licensees who fail to comply.

*Where principals appear in this statement, it refers also to assistant principals, vice principals, and deans (where the role is that of administrative support to the principal).

Resource D

STUDENT/PARENT/PRINCIPAL CONTRACT FOR
ELIMINATING GUNS AND WEAPONS FROM SCHOOLS

Guns and other weapons clearly are a hazard to a safe learning environment and the welfare of human beings. According to the National Center for Health Statistics, every day 14 young people, age 19 and under, are killed as a result of gun use. According to the Metropolitan Life Survey of American Teachers, 1993: Violence in America's Public Schools, 11% of teachers and 23% of students say they have been victims of violence in or near their schools. While the elimination of guns and weapons from schools is the responsibility of all segments of the school and society, three individuals have especially crucial responsibility: the student, the principal, and the parent. This contract draws attention to the specific responsibilities of those three individuals.

WE, THE UNDERSIGNED, AGREE TO THE FOLLOWING COMMITMENTS:

STUDENT
- I agree not to bring a gun or any weapon to school or to any school event.
- I will tell my peers to seek adult assistance when conflict situations begin to get out of control.
- I will not carry another person's gun or weapon.
- If I see a gun or other weapon on campus or at a school event, I will alert an adult about its existence.

        Student Signature _____

PARENT/GUARDIAN
- I will teach, including my personal example, my teenagers about the dangers and consequences of guns and weapons use, and I will keep any guns and all weapons I own under lock and away from my children.
- I will support the school's policies to eliminate guns and weapons and work with the school in developing programs to prevent violence.
- I will carry out my responsibility to teach my children how to settle arguments without resorting to violence, to encourage him/her to use those ideas when necessary, and to follow school guidelines for reporting guns and weapons they see to an appropriate adult.

        Parent Signature _____

PRINCIPAL
- I will ensure that students have an anonymous way to report to an adult any guns or other weapons they see on campus.
- I will promote conflict resolution instruction for all students as part of the curriculum.
- I will communicate the school's policies on guns and weapons to all participants in the school community and focus on the responsibilities we all have.
- I will use the school's student leadership groups and student meetings to obtain ideas to develop a safe school environment.

- I will report all guns and other weapons violations to law enforcement officials, according to established procedures.

Principal Signature _____

Signed:

Student_____ Date _____

Parent_____ Date _____

Principal_____ Date _____

Developed by the National Association of Secondary School Principals

References

Barth, R. (1990). *Improving schools from within*. San Francisco: Jossey-Bass.

Bennis, W., & Nanus, B. (1985). *Leaders: The strategies for taking charge*. Boston: Allyn & Bacon.

Blythe, M. C., & Bradbury, P. M. (1993). Classroom by committee. *Educational Leadership, 50*(7), 56-58.

Bodinger-de Uriarte, C. (1991, December). The rise of hate crime on school campuses. *Phi Delta Kappa Research Bulletin*, pp. 1-6.

Bossert, S. T., Dwyer, D. C., Rowan, B., & Lee, G. V. (1992). The instructional management role of the principal. *Educational Administrative Quarterly, 18*(3), 34-64.

Burke, J. (1991). Teenagers, clothes, and gang violence. *Educational Leadership, 49*(1), 11-13.

Butterfield, G. E., & Turner, B. (Eds.). (1989). *Weapons in schools* (NSSC resource paper). Malibu, CA: National School Safety Center. (ERIC Document Reproduction Service No. ED 310 536)

Bybee, R. W., & Gee, E. G. (1982). The phenomenon of violence in schools. In *Violence, value, and justice in the schools* (pp. 105-120). Boston: Allyn & Bacon.

Cohen, S., & Wilson-Brewer, R. (1991). *Violence prevention for young adolescents: The state of the art of program evaluation.* New York: Carnegie Council on Adolescent Development Working Papers.

Comerford, D. L., & Jacobson, M. G. (1987, April). *Suspension—Capital punishment for misdemeanors: The use of suspension at four suburban junior high schools and viable alternatives that could work.* Paper presented at the annual meetings of the American Educational Research Association, Washington, DC.

Cultice, W. W. (1992). Establishing an effective crisis intervention program. *NASSP Bulletin, 76*(543), 68-72.

David, J. L. (1989). Synthesis of research on school-based management. *Educational Leadership, 46*(8), 45-54.

Dodge, K. A. (1992). Youth violence: Who? What? Where? When? How? Why? *Tennessee Teacher, 60*(2), 9-11, 30.

Ecksel, I. B. (1992). The long and short of it. *Tennessee Teacher, 60*(2), 15-16, 27-29.

Eitzen, D. S. (1992). Problem students: The sociocultural roots. *Phi Delta Kappan, 73*(8), 584-590.

Fish, S. (1993, January 31). Student on the outs may stay in. *Orlando Sentinel,* pp. A-1, 8.

Flax, E. (1992, May-June). A time to mourn. *Teacher,* pp. 18-19.

Foley, D. (1990, May). Danger: School zone. *Teacher,* pp. 57-63.

Friedlander, B. Z. (1993). We can fight violence in the schools. *The Education Digest, 59*(2), 11-14.

Frisby, D., & Beckham, J. (1993). Dealing with violence and threats of violence in the school. *NASSP Bulletin, 77*(552), 10-15.

Garbarino, J., Dubrow, N., Kostelny, K., & Pardo, C. (1992). *Children in danger.* San Francisco: Jossey-Bass.

Gaustad, J. (1991). Schools respond to gangs and violence. *OSSC Bulletin, 34*(9), 1-54.

Gersten, R., Carnine, D., & Green, S. (1982). The principal as instructional leader: A second look. *Educational Leadership, 40*(3), 15-18.

Glasser, W. (1990). The quality school. *Phi Delta Kappan, 71*(6), 425-435.

Glatthorn, A. (1992). *Teachers as agents of change: A new look at school improvement.* Washington, DC: NEA Professional Library.

Greenbaum, S., & Turner, B. (Eds.). (1989). *Safe schools overview* (NSSC resource paper). Mailbu, CA: U.S. Department of Justice, U.S. Department of Education, & Pepperdine University.

Hahn, A. (1987). Reaching out to America's dropouts: What to do? *Phi Delta Kappan, 69*(4), 256-263.

Hammond, W. R. (1990). *Positive adolescents choices training (PACT): Preliminary findings of the effects of a school-based violence prevention program for African American adolescents.* Columbus: Ohio State Commission on Minority Health. (ERIC Document Reproduction Service No. ED 326 812)

Harrington-Lueker, D. (1992a). Blown away by school violence. *The American School Board Journal, 179*(5), 20-26.

Harrington-Lueker, D. (1992b). Metal detectors. *The American School Board Journal, 179*(5), 26-27.

Heath, S. B., & McLoughlin, M. W. (1987). A child resource policy: Moving beyond dependence on school and family. *Phi Delta Kappan, 68*(8), 576-580.

Henderson, A. T. (1987). *The evidence continues to grow: Parent involvement improves student achievement.* Columbia, MD: National Committee for Citizens in Education.

Henderson, A. T. (1988). Parents are a school's best friend. *Phi Delta Kappan, 70*(2), 148-153.

Hill, M. S. (1993). Opening doors for transient students. *Principal, 72*(3), 48-49.

Hill, M. S., & Simmons, M. (1993). Teachers as leaders: Fostering future decision makers. *DESIGN for Leadership, 3*(3), 2-8.

Hofferth, S. L. (1987). Implications of family trends for children: A research perspective. *Educational Leadership, 44*(5), 78-84.

Huelskamp, R. M. (1993). Perspectives on education in America. *Phi Delta Kappan, 74*(9), 718-725.

Jackson, B. L., & Cooper, B. S. (1992). Involving parents in improving urban schools. *NASSP Bulletin, 76*(543), 30-38.

Jennings, J. M. (1992). Parent involvement strategies for inner-city schools. *NASSP Bulletin, 76*(548), 63-68.

Johnson, W. O. (1993). The agony of victory. *Sports Illustrated, 79*(1), pp. 30-37.

Kadel, S., & Follman, J. (1993). *Reducing school violence.* Tallahassee, FL: SouthEastern Regional Vision for Education.

Landen, W. (1992). Violence and our schools: What can we do? *Updating School Board Policies, 23*(1), 1-5.

LaPoint, V., Holloman, L. O., & Alleyne, S. I. (1992). The role of dress codes, uniforms in urban schools. *NASSP Bulletin, 76*(546), 20-26.

Lawton, M. (1993, May 5). Anywhere, at any time. Violence in school spread past cities. *Education Week,* pp. 1, 14.

Lysted, M. (Ed.). (1986). *Violence in the home: Interdisciplinary perspectives.* New York: Brunner/Mazel.

Melaville, A. I., & Blank, M. J. (1993). *Together we can.* Washington, DC: Government Printing Office.

Memphis City Schools. (1993, April 2). *Report of the school violence task force.* Memphis: Author.

Michael, B. (Ed.). (1990). *Volunteers in public schools.* Washington, DC: National Academy Press.

Modglin, T. (1989, Spring). School crime: Up close and personal. *School Safety,* pp. 9-11.

Moriarty, A., & Fleming, T. W. (1990). Youth gangs aren't just a big-city problem anymore. *The Executive Educator, 12*(7), 13-16.

National Institute of Education. (1978). *Violent schools—safe schools: The safe schools study report to Congress.* Washington, DC: Government Printing Office.

National School Safety Center. (1990). *School crisis prevention and response.* Malibu, CA: Author.

Northern, T. K., & Bailey, G. D. (1991). Instructional leaders for the 21st century: Seven critical characteristics. *Educational Considerations, 18*(2), 25-28.

O'Neil, J. (1991). A generation adrift. *Educational Leadership, 49*(1), 4-9.

Orange County Public Schools. (1993). *Pocket fact sheet.* Orlando, FL: Author.

Ordovensky, P. (1993). Facing up to violence. *The Executive Educator, 15*(1), 22-24.

Pines, M. (1980, December). Psychological hardiness. *Psychology Today,* pp. 34-44, 98.

Prophet, M. (1990). Safe schools in Portland. *The American School Board Journal, 177*(10), 28-30.

Purkey, S. C., & Smith, M. S. (1982). Too soon to cheer? Synthesis of research on effective schools. *Educational Leadership, 40*(3), 64-69.

Pynoos, R., & Nader, K. (1988). Psychological first aid and treatment approach to children exposed to community violence. *Journal of Traumatic Stress, 1*(4), 445-473.

Quarles, C. (1989). *School violence: A survival guide for school staff with emphasis on robbery, rape, and hostage taking.* West Haven, CT: National Educational Association Professional Library.

Research Action Brief. (1981). *Violence in the schools: How much? What to do?* Eugene, OR: ERIC Clearinghouse on Educational Management.

Rich, J. M. (1992). Predicting and controlling school violence. *Contemporary Education, 64*(1), 35-39.

Rossilini, R. (1988). *A parents' guide to drug abuse, prevention, and treatment.* Miami: John Alden Life Insurance Company.

Rutter, M., Maughan, B., Mortimer, P., Ouston, J., & Smith, A. (1979). *Fifteen thousand hours: Secondary schools and their effects on children.* Cambridge, MA: Harvard University Press.

Shoop, R. L., & Dunklee, D. R. (1992). *School law for the principal: A handbook for practitioners.* Needham Heights, MA: Allyn & Bacon.

Sinclair, E., & Alexson, J. (1992). Relationship of behavioral characteristics to educational needs. *Behavioral Disorders, 17*(4), 292-304.

Smith, D. (1989). The Cleveland elementary school shooting. *Thrust, 18*(7), 8-11.

Steinberg, A. (1991). How schools can help stem violence in today's youth. *Educational Digest,* pp. 40-43.

Stover, D. (1988). School violence is rising, and your staff is the target. *The Executive Educator, 10*(10), 15-21, 33.

Thirty-one percent of parents worry about guns in school. (1993, June 23). *Education Week,* p. 2.

Toby, J. (1983). *Violence in schools.* Washington, DC: U.S. Department of Justice, National Institute of Justice.

U.S. Department of Health and Human Services. (1993). *The prevention of youth violence: A framework for community action.* Atlanta: Centers for Disease Control and Prevention.

Wheeler, N. (1989, September). *A motivational behavioral approach to violence in school.* Paper presented at the National Conference of the Council for Exceptional Children, Charlotte, NC. (ERIC Document Reproduction Service No. ED 315 983)

Winters, A. T. (1992). Youth violence and drug use/abuse: How do they fit together? *Tennessee Teacher, 60*(2), 25-26.

Woodall, M. V., & Bond, J. (1993, October). Showing up and doing well. *The Executive Educator, 15,* 25-27.

Zajdel, H. A. (1993). How to organize and keep school volunteers. *NASSP Bulletin, 77*(553), 107-109.

Index

Smith, Marshall S., 16, 70
Sports, 1, 12
Staten Island Project, 61
Stover, Del, 45, 98, 102
Students
    apparel, 103
    at risk, 63, 78, 88
    dropouts, 44, 73, 74
    participate, 48, 53
    rights, responsibilities, 48
Substance abuse. *See* Chemical
    dependency
Suicide, 44, 79
Superintendent. *See* Leadership
Suspension, 46, 47, 88

Teachers
    aides, 34, 38, 101
    as leaders, 35, 72
    competent, 37, 81
    permanent substitutes, 81
    strategies, 28, 33, 78, 79, 98

Technology, 34, 37, 76, 96, 99, 108,
    109
Teen pregnancy, 4, 30
Time on task, 32, 33
Toby, Jackson, 21
Transportation, 80, 108
Turner, Brenda, 20, 36, 100

Unemployment, 4, 64, 74
United States Department of Health
    and Human Services, 52

Volunteers, 34, 49, 55, 57, 61, 62, 63,
    64, 67

Weapons, 6, 7, 8, 9, 14, 44, 98, 103
Wheeler, Nedra, 115
Wilson-Brewer, Renee, 44
Winters, Anita, 10, 11
Woodall, Michael, 33

Zajdel, Heidi, A., 66